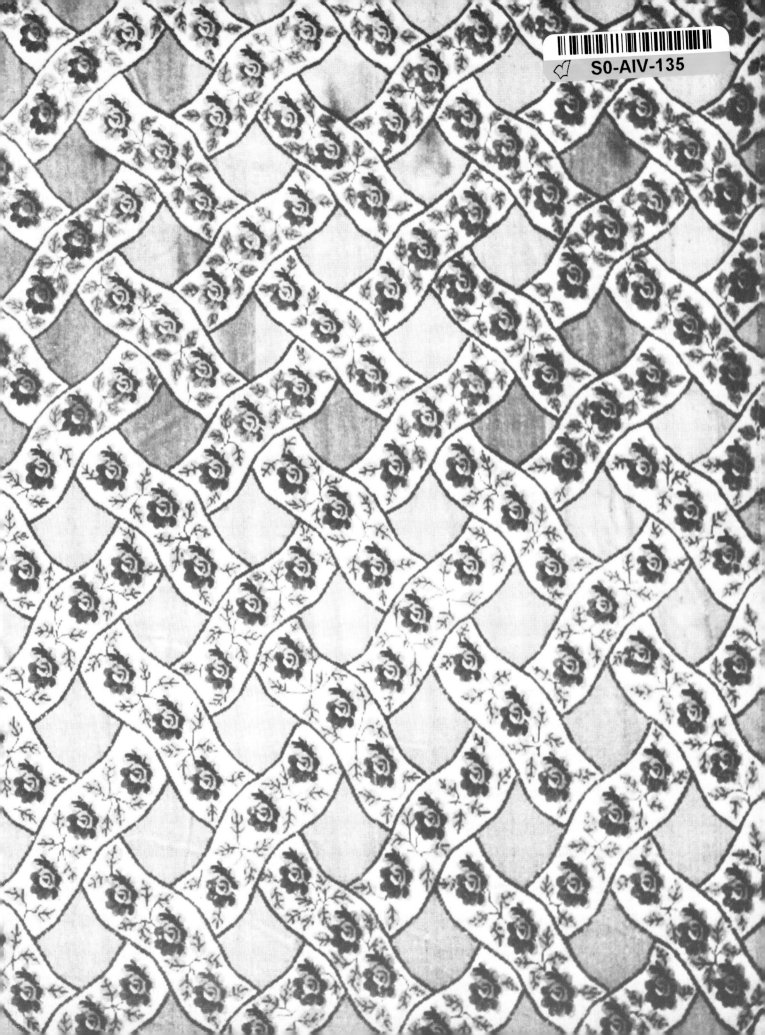

American Rugs and Carpets

American Rugs and Carpets

From the Seventeenth Century to Modern Times

Helene Von Rosenstiel

William Morrow and Company, Inc.
New York

Library of Congress Catalog Card Number 78-50700
ISBN 0-688-03325-3

Produced by Walter Parrish International Limited, London
Designed by Victor Giolitto

Set in 11 on 13 pt Ehrhardt
Printed and bound in Great Britain by Purnell & Sons Limited

Contents

Author's Acknowledgements

Writing this book has given me a unique opportunity to explore an aspect of the American decorative arts which has traditionally received short shrift. Perhaps this is because few examples of rugs and carpets exist and many pattern books have disappeared as corporations have merged, failed or burned. However, goldmines of information do exist and much of it has been made accessible to me through the generosity of numerous people, institutions and corporations.

I wish to thank all the people who shared with me the enthusiasm of discovery, encouraged me in this project and generously gave of their time. Many people's recollections of what decorative coverings were on their floors, how they cared for them, how they felt about the carpeting or linoleum rugs, have added new dimensions to my understanding. I wish to thank all the museums and curators who granted me access to their collections of floor coverings and paintings, to their libraries and photo archives, and permitted illustration of their treasures. Many thanks are due to the dealers and collectors who helped find related materials, and allowed their personal collections to be photographed, and to the floor covering corporations and their staffs who provided samples, promotional material, unpublished histories, photography, access to archives, and patient explanations of complicated technical processes, pattern and design trends.

I wish to especially thank Iain MacDonald, Director of Weaving, The Bigelow Sanford Corporation; Katherine Koob, Assistant Curator, Merrimac Valley Textile Museum; and Dick Sinclair, The Armstrong Corporation, for reading and advising on the manuscript; Richard Kressler of Magee Carpets for his thoughtful insights; Wendell Thomas and The Carpet and Rug Institute for permitting attendance at their training school; Peggy Zorach, Head Librarian, The Brooklyn Museum, for granting special research privileges; Gary and Cyndy Reynolds for their unending support and encouragement; Phoebe Phillips and the staff of Walter Parrish International Ltd., who produced the book; Mel Wathen and James Viola, my special photographers; Ann George for her beautiful drawings; Irene Gavin and Marty Von Rosenstiel for the expert typing of endless letters and manuscript pages, and my mother, Marion Von Rosenstiel, who was my thoughtful research assistant and editor.

Introduction

The history of floor coverings in America is the history of America itself. It is the story of immigration and migration, imitation, changes in American taste, invention and industrial adaptation. Above all, it reflects one aspect of the American dream of a better life.

Carpets have always been a rather neglected area of the American decorative arts—a stepped-on child of American cultural history. Only in recent years has there been any interest in the preservation, collection or use of floor coverings of all kinds. The general concern to preserve America's architectural heritage has been largely responsible for the recognition of carpets as a significant part of interior decoration.

This book presents a survey of many kinds of floor treatments used in America—from decorated dirt floors to AstroTurf, from floorcloths and oilcloths to vinyl tiles, from hand-made rugs to machine-made carpets. (The difference between a carpet and a rug is often not very clear: sometimes the terms are used interchangeably but on the whole a carpet can be defined as "a soft floor covering installed wall-to-wall and fastened down" and a rug as "a floor covering of any size or material finished on all four sides that does not cover an entire floor and can be laid without being fastened down.") In such a wide survey, each type of floor covering must, of necessity, be treated with brevity. Sometimes educated guesses will have to suffice where a paucity of original examples makes collecting information difficult. More than any other of the decorative arts, carpets have a tendency to wear out or become outmoded and when they did, in the past, they were often cut up, cut down for other uses, thrown away, or reconstituted into other carpet forms. But fortunately many floor coverings have been documented in numerous American genre paintings, photographs and advertisements. From these we can ascertain trends in colors and patterns, even if it is not possible to tell from these sources alone what a floor covering actually was, or how it was made, unless a period caption specifically says so, since costly fashionable floor treatments have always been imitated in various substitute forms. Besides helping to fill in the gaps, this kind of documentation, together with a familiarity with the various stages in the development of the carpet industry, is extremely valuable in helping us to identify the many existing examples, whether whole or fragments.

In today's extensively carpeted environment, people seldom notice what is under foot, and even if they are conversant with current trends and aware of historic hand-crafted carpet forms, they may not realize that both are part of a long, continuous evolution. *American Rugs and Carpets* shows how each step in this evolution came about and how it was a step nearer the fulfilment of the American dream of a carpet for every floor.

1 Alternate Floors

The old rug making skills of the Middle East had already migrated once—through Spain and France and England—as the result of centuries of exploration, conquest, colonization, religious persecution and trade, well before the shores of the New World were first explored and colonized. Rugs had long been a luxury of the aristocracy by the time the first settlers came to the New World.

Some of the settlers who migrated from the 17th century onwards brought with them limited items of luxury and the decorative traditions of their homelands. Some came with only the barest necessities; some brought with them also recollections of straw matting, tiled or parquet floors, table carpets or embroidered rugs. Some brought skills from the homelands—weaving, spinning, dyeing—taught through generations of the master apprenticeship system. But the earliest came to a land where the earth was the floor, and a skin or a mat was a luxurious covering (and remained so for many pioneers throughout the 19th century). It was not long, however, before settlers throughout America began to improve on the plain, tamped earth, adapting their own traditions and local materials to provide comfort and beauty.

Before there could be carpets, there had to be floors to put them on. Dirt mixed with other ingredients was one of the oldest forms of flooring used throughout America. Those in the east may well have evolved from the warm, durable clay and dirt floors in common use in England about 1753 described by Isaac Ware, in *A Complete Body of Architecture*. "The common floors used in mean buildings, are made of loam well beaten and tempered with smith's dust (from anvil), and with or without an addition of lime. Some also make them of pure clay, oxblood (and stale milk), and a moderate portion of sharp sand; these three ingredients beaten together very thoroughly, and well spread, make a firm and good floor; and of a beautiful colour."[1] Such a floor could be polished to a high gloss if rubbed immediately with a woolen cloth.

Few floors of the type known as "ash-lime floors" still exist. A Williamsburg researcher did find one on an upper story in the Herr House of 1719 in Lancaster County, Pennsylvania. The base material was of sticks covered with reeds or straw before the plaster was applied.[2] It may well be that others still lie hidden under later floorboards.

Floors for elegant houses, according to Isaac Ware, were made of stucco—plaster of Paris beaten, sifted and mixed with other ingredients that created various colors.

Floors made with oxblood were brown when very new but ultimately turned light gray. Those with yellow ochre added to the mixture had a pale buff color. Some of the solid-color floors in American primitive paintings may well be of these types; however, since other colors besides the buff and pale gray do appear, it is possible that they may have been painted boards instead.

In the 18th century, a traveler to Florida described the houses as having "a very singular appearance within being floored with a kind of reddish stucco, intermixed with shells instead of planks . . . performed by the Spanish during their settlement . . . washed clean every day."[3] In Florida, the red stucco floors, similar in appearance to the red and white terazzo often used in Florida houses today, were cool and bug proof. They were probably a matter of choice, since lumber, reeds and rushes were most likely readily available.

In the Southwest, however, dirt floors in the adobe houses of the early Spanish settlers were a necessity more than a reflection and adaptation of an existing tradition. Climate severely limited materials and the scarce lumber was needed to provide rafters for the roof. Many oxblood dirt floors, with a rich patina of time and use, remain in houses throughout the Southwest, some dating back about three hundred years. Many of these dwellings are still inhabited, but health and building codes no longer permit the building of new floors of this type.

Board floors were one of the first improvements to the tamped earth. They were used in some of the earliest shelters dug into hillsides by the early colonists in New England and New York[4] and have been a satisfactory flooring ever since—as a base for decorative treatments worked directly on them and as a surface on which to place or to set off carpets. Floorboards were used to make the house warmer and easier to keep clean, just as the ash-lime and oxblood floors were. With the vast quantities of dirt and mud tracked into the houses from the street or farmyard, keeping a house clean was a problem. Sand was used for generations as a cleaning material, in combination with water, a scrub brush and elbow grease, to scour the floor. When the floor was clean and dry, the sand could be swept away. Recipes as late as 1890 in domestic household books provide explicit cleaning instructions, including bleaching instructions which are carried out after the scrubbing is finished.[5] Floors scrubbed for years in this manner usually retained the color of light, new wood. They had a ribbed texture created by areas where the soft wood had been worn away, leaving raised ribs of hard graining. Some were scrubbed so often that the boards had holes in them.

Philipsburg Manor, an early-18th-century Dutch house/mill in Tarrytown, New York, has been restored and cleaned with traditional scouring methods, giving the entire interior a bright clean look. It is an excellent example of the way many of the interiors of early American houses, at least in the New York area, may have looked.

Numerous references in letters and journals show that sand was also used as a kind of floor covering, a type of substitute carpet. Fine sand was dug from a nearby stream or, in some cities, purchased from a sandman. This was a long-standing custom in America. As early as 1746 a William Wheeler advertised in the *Boston News-Letter* that he had ". . . scouring sand for Floors . . . The Larger the Quantity the less the Price."[6] Sand was sprinkled on the floors with a sieve, or put in little piles and then swept about to cover the floors. Wet sand was not as dusty as the dry, and easier to control, just as the damp sawdust in butcher shops or janitor's cleaning powder is today.[7]

One such room with an even covering of sand carpet was described by an 18th-century lady as "a white floor sprinkled with clean sand, large tables and heavy high back chairs of walnut or mahogany . . . [which] . . . decorated a parlour genteely enough for anybody . . ."[8] or almost anybody. Even in houses of the middle class, floors were sanded in the better rooms. The Philadelphia historian Watson described this process in more detail. "Parlour floors of very respectable people in business used to be swept and garnished every morning with sand sifted through a 'sand sieve,' and sometimes smoothed with a hair broom into quaint circles and fancy wreaths, agreeably to the 'Genius for drawing' possessed by the chamber maid."[9] Sand floors were genteel and respectable enough for almost everybody, except ". . . the rich" who by 1781 were ". . . covering their floors with woolen carpets or rush matting and others with fine sand."[10] Although sand in such designs provided only temporary patterns, set in disarray by a single footstep, it served a dual purpose—to aid in keeping the house clean and to make a pretty, patterned floor or threshhold "door mat."

This once-popular floor covering has long since sifted through the cracks in the floor or been swept through the door, its history traced only in letters and journals, and documented by sandpiles found under the floorboards.

Was paint originally used to make floors easier to clean, to make them prettier, to use up remnants of paint, to make a smooth surface free of splinters, or to imitate a finer floor covering? Exactly when or why board floors began to be painted in early America is unknown. It is known that in London, in 1739, a pattern book entitled *Various Kinds of Floor Decorations Represented Both in Plano and Perspective Being Useful Designs for Ornamenting the Floors of Halls, Rooms, Summer Houses, etc., in Twenty Four Copper Plates. Designed and Engraved by John Carwitham* was published, and undoubtedly had its effect on American floor decoration.

It is also known that paints were available for indoor use after 1725, and that merchants advertised long lists of colors and painter's supplies in many cities by 1760—among them Benjamin Hawes, a Charleston merchant who offered nearly 100 items.[11]

Certainly by 1790 paints *were* being used on the floor. Ralph Earl carefully recorded (in his portrait of Uriah Tracy) not only a simple geometric floor-pattern in red, gray-green and black, but also the cracks between the boards.[12] From then on it begins to be possible to document floors more specifically through remnants of colors and patterns found on floors which—these still existed many years later—confirm many of the colors and suggest patterns which appear frequently in genre paintings.

Some floors were painted in solid colors: dark reddish brown, green, grays, yellow ochre, and blue.[13] Others were decorated by freehand painting, stencil, marbleizing, or spatter paint. In most cases there was a visual difference between the freedom of hand painting and the formal, sharp-edged patterning of stenciling but the quality of either depended upon the skill of the painter—often an itinerant craftsman.

Top: "John and Abigail Montgomery" painted by Joseph H. Davis, 1836. *Center:* "Caverly Family of Stafford, New Hampshire" painted by Joseph H. Davis, 1836. *Bottom:* "James and Sarah Tuttle" painted by Joseph H. Davis, 1836.

Three almost identical family portraits showing the spectacular patterned floors so characteristic of the Joseph H. Davis watercolors. The scale is greatly enlarged. The extensive use of blue in the patterns—not a frequent color—suggests freehand-painted floors based on fashionable carpets.

Freehand designs were applied to a solid-colored background with brushes or sponges according to the whim and imagination of the painter. Some like those in the familiar genre paintings of Joseph H. Davis, a popular, prolific itinerant artist of the 1830s, may have been either representations of carpets or fabulous imaginary floor coverings. Others were known to have been painted with elaborate landscapes. The fine painted staircase from the 1781 Weathersfield White House has blue painted steps with olive green "vines" or "rock crevices" flanking either side of a green painted stair runner. It is a good example of freehand brush painting and is still to be seen in the H. F. du Pont Winterthur collection at Winterthur, Delaware. A sponge-painted example is in the Dutton House in Shelburne, Vermont (see illustration).

Stenciled floors created precise and repeated patterns which frequently copied the figures in fashionable carpets. Specific directions "to Paint in Figures For Carpets Or Borders" were included in *A Select Collection of Valuable and Curious Arts and Interesting Experiments*, published in 1825 by Rufus Porter, an itinerant painter, inventor and journalist. Instructions included how to cut stencils and apply the paint to a floor or floor cloth.[14]

Freehand-painted floor in Dutton House (after 1782). It has a random pattern in dark brown applied with a sponge to gray.

Characteristic type of stenciled border pattern, taken from South Deerfield House, Deerfield, Massachusetts.

There is a stenciled floor imitating an ingrain carpet pattern of that period in the Bump Tavern at Cooperstown, New York. Another, with a reddish-brown carpet pattern stenciled on a yellow-gold background, was discovered in Dorchester, Massachusetts. One also has been found which combines a free-hand central pattern of painted black and natural wood diamonds with stenciled border of tulips that resembles patterns of both floorcloths and tile floors. Many of the other patterns were clear, simple, decorative repeated designs.

Marbled floors that became popular with the neo-classic revival in the 18th and early 19th centuries were painted to imitate real marble. Geometric blocks of gray or black and white often had veining applied with a feather. The geometric patterns were fairly simple to lay out on the floor and paint freehand, and sometimes included borders and classical motifs. Several of the floors were actually found in Nantucket, Massachusetts and other coastal towns in the 1930s.[15] Those in genre paintings could be painted floors, like the floor in the well known "Child with Dog" from the Abby Aldrich Rockefeller Folk Art Collection. A similar design in black, white, burnt sienna and ochre was once painted on an early-19th-century floor in Mystic, Connecticut. According to

Painted floor pattern in a three-dimensional perspective with neoclassical motifs from a house in Mystic, Connecticut.

Painted-board floor at Van Cortlandt Manor, Tarrytown, New York, in a black and light gray geometric pattern. It clearly shows veining in imitation of marble.

legend the owner of the house suffered from asthma and believed that he would be unable to sleep in a room containing any carpeting, so he provided a substitute for his floor and peace of mind.[16]

Spatter-painted floors, which used drops of random-colored paint on a solid-colored background, had long been considered a colonial form, until the 1930s, when Esther Stevens Fraser, who extensively researched painted and stenciled floors, commented that she had ". . . yet to see traces of a really ancient spatter floor . . . if spatter dates prior to 1840 it is strange that we have encountered no earlier traces of it." She suspected that spatter floors originated in the Victorian era.[17]

Painted floors continued in use throughout the 19th century. Freehand painted and stenciled carpet patterns began to disappear as real carpets became more widely available. Instead, painted floors often simulated the fashionable and costly parquet which came into vogue in the second half of the 19th century. One example at the Speedwell Village Restoration, Morristown, New Jersey, may have been inspired by the extravagant striped parquet at Lyndhurst, the home of Jay Gould in Tarrytown, New York. Another, painted to resemble patterned parquet, was discovered during recent renovation in the 1870s residence of a wealthy 19th-century Cincinnati brewer, John Hauck. Elaborate wooden parquet on the parlor floor, installed about 1880, had replaced the less elegant painted imitation.

Many old painted floors may still be discovered during the widespread restoration and renovation of old houses—protected by later wooden or resilient floorings. Other evidence may point to the original use of sand, ash-lime or oxblood, the floorings of an earlier time. Today, new floors are being painted in the old patterns, some by the owners themselves, and some by professional itinerant artisans. But these floors, painted or stenciled in decorative patterns, continue the tradition of one alternate floor in America.

Mid-19th-century painted floor simulating parquet at the Speedwell Village Restoration. The even light and dark stripes do not match up with the cracks in the slightly irregular floorboards.

Corner detail of elaborate 1880s parquet which replaced earlier painted parquet in the parlor of the John Hauck House in Cincinnati, Ohio.

2 Matting

Straw and rush matting was one of the earliest, most popular, versatile, and economical floor coverings in continuous use in America. Yet, it is one of the least documented. Perhaps, over the years, it received little mention in household journals and accounts precisely because it was inexpensive (and, therefore, often a poor-man's substitute for more luxurious carpeting), perhaps because it was versatile (and, therefore, taken for granted as a protective covering for "good rugs" or areas of hard wear).

Though the earliest settlers probably followed European cottage tradition and simply covered the floors of their first crude dwellings with grass, rushes, or pine boughs, they must have begun to use matting soon afterwards. It was already well known in England, as 17th-century paintings and writings indicate, and was an excellent insulator against both heat and cold. Mats "to lye under 50 bedds aboard shippe" were, in fact, listed on the manifest when Governor Endicott came to Massachusetts in 1628.[1] Similar natural materials for making matting—grasses, reeds, bark and rush—were certainly readily available in the New World. By the time the earliest settlers came, the tribes of woodland Indians inhabiting the area had a tradition of mat-weaving for their long houses—weaving and plaiting mats on the simplest upright looms. In 1630

Quarter-inch-wide strips of light and dark cedar bark woven into a patterned matting: Eastern Woodlands Indians.

Plaited rush matting in
characteristic diagonal pattern:
Eastern Woodlands Indians.

Woven grass matting with a
warp of basswood fiber cords.

Opposite:
Shuttleworth Brothers "Karnak"
Wilton rug, sold through W. &
J. Sloane in 1918. The softness
of the image due to the pile is
revealed in this close-up view.
The Liberty rug was designed
as a promotional item and
depicts historic landmarks, state
seals, transportation and
industry.

Reverend Francis Higginson described, in his *New Englands Plantation,* Indian
wigwams as "verie little and homely . . . matted with boughs and covered with
sedge and old mats."[2] Just as the early Massachusetts settlers copied those
Indian wigwams—as frequent references to "English wigwams" attest—they
probably learned to make matting or obtained it by barter from the Indians.
They may even have developed a limited home manufacture. Widespread use
is difficult to trace, however, before the mid-18th century since inventories and
writings of travelers fail to mention matting before then.

That mat-making was an established English craft is reflected in a 1720
notice in the *London Gazette* No. 5891/4 which announces that "Thomas

Matting loom used by the
Eastern Woodlands Indians.

Smith . . . of that branch called a matted-chair-maker, is in want of Journey-
men . . . for matting."[3] With growing trade, increasing quantities of matting
were also imported via England from India and China. Numerous advertisements of the period report new wares for purchase, sometimes in as little as
twenty days after shipment from England. Trade was brisk and housewares of
all kinds, undoubtedly including matting, may often have reached American
ports even before reaching many elegant English residences.

In the 1750s, Israel Acrelius, Royal representative to the Swedish congrega-
tion on the Delaware River near Philadelphia, commented that "straw carpets
have lately been introduced to the towns. But the inconvenience of this is that
they must soon be cleansed from flyspots, and a multitude of vermin which
harbor in such things, and from kitchen smoke, which is universal."[4]

Importation of the mattings continued through the 1750s via England.
Imported into Norfolk, Virginia, by Balfour and Barraud in 1766 were "floor
cloth . . . painted floor cloths . . . door mats . . . matting, etc."[5] During the
1760s George Washington purchased vast quantities for Mount Vernon
through his agents, Robert Cary, Esq. & Company, including "50 yards of
best floor matting" which he used in his formal banquet room.[6] Although the
original has long been worn out, the room has been refurbished with semi-hand-
woven tatami matting from Japan, the yard-wide strips sewn together and the
entire bound in dark brown. According to inventories, matting was used in
other parts of the mansion. It was imported from England and made, perhaps,
of rush.

The Townsend Non-Importation Acts of 1767 limited trade with England,
thereby encouraging trade within the colonies. By the 1780s the American
merchants' clipper ships were trading directly with China. In 1789 George

Opposite:
"Two Women" painted by
Eunice Pinney, first quarter of
the 19th century. The linear
geometric patterns which cover
the entire floor are reminiscent
of John Carwitham's
recommended instruction for the
design of painted floor coverings
which should be "Both in Plano
and Perspective. . ."

"The Prodigal's Return" *c.* 1835–40, showing matting or straw-patterned floorcloth used as a protective covering for a wall-to-wall patterned green carpet.

Washington was again refurbishing Mount Vernon, but this time through Robert Morris of Philadelphia, whom he thanked for "the obliging attention which you have given to the Floor matting from China."[7]

Matting or straw carpets, far from being relegated to attics or less important rooms, were a fashionable and popular floor covering throughout much of the 19th century. Grass, rush or straw matting was used not only as a protective covering for "good carpets" but was put down after the good wool carpets were cleaned, rolled and put away for the summer.

A recollection of 1828 by Edward Everett Hale describes this seasonal ritual: "Carpets then of English make, covered the whole floor, and were of what we should now call perfect quality. In summer, by the way, in all houses of which I knew anything, these carpets were always taken up and India matting substituted in the 'living rooms.' Observe that very few houses were closed in summer."[8]

Perhaps more importantly, in 1869 the use of matting was encouraged by Catherine E. Beecher, a prolific mid-19th century writer on Domestic Science, as an economical, practical way to beautify the parlor of a simple home. Instead of spending $80 for a "very homely Brussels carpet . . ." which would have outlasted several ordinary ingrains, she recommended covering the floor

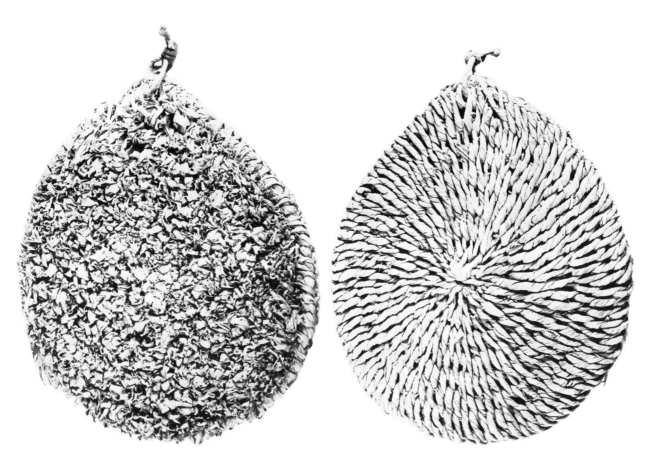

Left and right:
Front and back of a
corn husk mat. Husks were
braided into mats on countless
American farms to make a useful
product from an easily available
material.

with "thirty yards of good matting, at fifty cents a yard" (a fifteen-dollar carpet which permitted buying wallpaper, curtains and pictures with the balance). She noted that matting was "not good economy in a dining-room or hard-worn sitting room" but was "precisely the thing for a parlor." One city parlor, in use summer and winter for seven years, was used for receiving "people who live upon velvet and Brussels" and was described as being ". . . a very attractive room."[9]

Fortunately, the use of matting as a carpet also preserved at least one earlier painted floor, stenciled in a carpet pattern.

Mattings were made of various natural fibers: sedge, flags, rushes, coir (or coconut husks), hemp, jute, or corn husks. Sedge is a tufted marsh plant with a solid stem. Flags are long-leaved reeds such as cattail and iris. In 1846 "Flag Carpets" were noted in the account book of Sister Joanna Kitchell of the New Lebanon Shaker Community.[10] Rushes are long-leaved, hollow-stemmed swamp plants, the leaves of which are also used in the manufacture of chair seats.

Husks, the dried outer covering of corn, were often braided into doormats, leaving a rough textured surface on the top. The instructions for "Mats (husk)—to make" in *What Every One Should Know* are amusingly characteristic of late-19th-century domestic encyclopedias, and merit quoting in full:

A good respectable-looking husk mat is not an unsightly looking object, and I wish all housekeepers knew what a world of scrubbing and wiping of floors it saved, that they might have one. One bushel basket and a boiler full of husks is sufficient to braid a large mat. If you have boys or girls, it will be fun for them to braid one in the evening; but, if like myself, you have neither, it would pay you to take the time and do it yourself. Have ready a teakettle full of hot water and turn into the boiler of husks. Begin a common three-strand braid, and as you bring over a strand place about three husks on; leave the large ends of the husks up. When enough is braided for a mat, sew firmly with twine in any shape you choose— long, round or oval. Then sprinkle warm water on the upper side. Run a fork through the husks, splintering the ends into a mass of little, curly fibers. Then, with the shears, trim off evenly. This can all be done in one evening by a good worker. I braid enough in the fall to last the year round.[11]

Jute, an Indian bast fiber that grows from 8 to 15 feet tall, was first extensively imported into England and America in the 1820s and used primarily for carpeting. Not until the 1870s was jute introduced by the Department of Agriculture into the United States where it was successfully grown only in limited quantities. The finest jute still comes from India and until recently was

Patterned and plain summer carpets used on a brick-floored porch in the June issue of 1918 of *Good Furniture Magazine*.

used both for porch or summer carpets and as the stuffer and backing in machine-made carpets.

Coir, or cocoa matting, is (despite its spelling) made from the spun fibers of coconut husks. An article in *The Carpet Trade* of 1877 offers this information on production: "All the yarn used for Coir matting is spun by the natives in the countries where cocoanuts grow. The first time Coir matting was ever used as a floor covering in any quantity was about twenty-six years ago [*sic*], in St. George's Hall, at Windsor, England, on the occasion of the christening of the Prince of Wales."[12]

Coir was a favorite for doormats. Sometimes it was flatwoven, but more frequently it had a coarse pile surface. It had astonishing wearing qualities, and the rough surface quickly removed mud from shoes. Some mats were solid in color, some were bordered with red, some late-19th-century ones known as "motto mats" were printed with messages that proclaimed "Welcome," "Good Day," or "Use Me." Although no longer available for $1.25, cocoa mats are still available and frequently used in the 1970s.

Throughout the 19th century and into the early 20th, frequent advertisements by Montgomery Ward and by Sears, Roebuck & Company, as well as by retailers of carpets, appeared for durable coarse-hemp or jute matting, available in 1877 in twill and herringbone weaves, in about 1895 in plain color or striped,

Advertisement for Chinese and Japanese matting available through Sears, Roebuck and Company, 1909. A wide variety of colors and patterns sharply differentiate the Chinese (*top*) and Japanese (*bottom*).

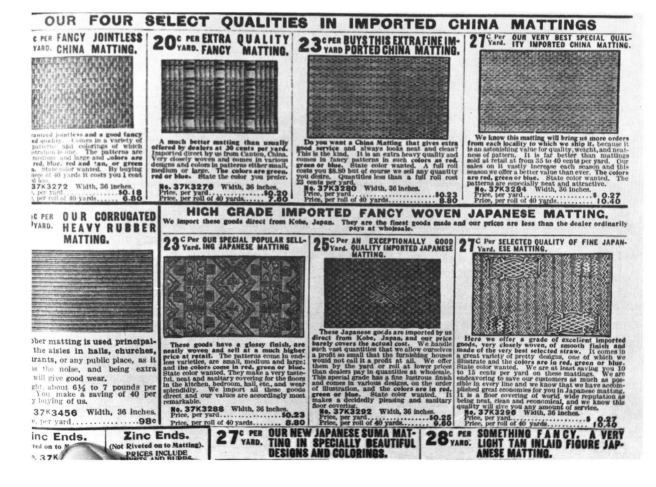

from 18 to 54 inches wide, from 18 to 76 cents a yard depending on quality and width. Hemp was also used for stair carpetings.

Calcutta matting, a durable, cheap variety, had an uneven weave and a drab color. Japanese and Chinese matting were other popular types.

> For health and comfort, no floor covering of the present day [1877] is so desirable, during the summer months, as a Chinese, Japanese, or East India matting. The first now comprises a great variety in design or color as well as quality. In selecting Chinese matting, broad cross stripes should be avoided, as they never match, and the necessary stretching produces a curvature of the pattern which is disagreeable to the eye. The plain natural color of the straw, the "checks"—red, green, chocolate and other colors—and the chenille patterns are the most desirable. The Japanese mattings are a lighter fabric, with a fragrance like prairie grass when fresh and new, and are very durable. The East India mattings are woven in squares, large enough to cover an ordinary room, and are very pretty with their alternating tints of pale straw and Indian Red.[13]

According to *The Carpet Trade* of June 1877, the Chinese matting was by far the best, since it always gave "just measure, no more and no less. A piece of 'Canton' matting will measure just forty yards; and the width, whether 'three-quarter,' 'four-quarter,' 'five-quarter,' or 'six-quarter,' is very exact . . . The best straws are used for the 'white mattings,' the inferior are colored."[14]

By the 1890s there was a definite difference in construction between Chinese and Japanese mattings. The Chinese were made with a manila-hemp warp and rush weft in either two- to five-yard pieces or in forty-yard single lengths. The Japanese matting was woven with a cotton warp and a rush weft and was more flexible.

In 1902 Sears offered Japanese matting, a bargain at 15 cents per yard, "in a beautiful Oriental coloring, the equal of matting that sells everywhere at 25 cents; and our 29-cent matting is a new number of our own importation, one of the heaviest, richest and most expensive mattings that has ever been shown, rich enough for any room, used largely for covering drawing rooms, parlors, etc., in some of the summer homes of millionaires." Predominant colors of the season were red, green, and blue, and others had "Japanese yellow and Oriental green stripe effect alternating."[15]

Grass rugs were also made domestically. In 1914 the Waite Grass Carpet Company advertised "Wire Grass Rugs" with a sun- and weatherproof warp, guaranteed colorfast. They were advertised as economical, artistic, and sanitary, and when no longer fresh and attractive could, as most matting, be put under carpets as padding.

Crex-trademarked carpets were another of the grass carpets manufactured domestically. They too were made from long-fiber wiregrass, native to the northwestern prairies, and were available with numerous patterns. In the 1920s, Crex "fiber rugs" became available. This type of inexpensive floor covering was constructed from yarns made from paper twirled around twine. The patterns were printed on, and as the surface wore off, the carpet was turned over to reveal the plain weave of the other side.

Matting presented problems not only of wear but of care. As early as 1750

Israel Acrelius noted that straw carpets were easily soiled by flyspecks and household dirt. Since this must have been a common problem, recipes were devised for the care of matting beyond routine sweeping or shaking. In 1845 the author of *How to Do Things Well and Cheap for Domestic Use* suggested that one "Wash them with a handful of Indian meal in the water; if very dirty, use it like sand; but do not use soap; it makes them yellow."[16] An 1888 recipe advises "washing twice a season with a warm solution made by dissolving a pint of salt in half a pailful of soft water, the object of the salt to prevent it from turning yellow. After washing, the matting should be quickly dried with a soft cloth, or hung out of doors on a line to dry."[17] Housewives were also warned not to allow drops of water to dry on the surface since that might leave hard-to-remove spots; and that varnish on heavy furniture might become soft in warm weather and stain the matting. A thin coat of varnish, applied to straw matting, however, would make it more durable and keep it looking fresh. At the turn of the century, matting of various types was widely used as an alternative to carpeting in dining rooms, halls, and bedrooms of summer cottages, and year-round houses. Examples are frequently illustrated in the magazines of that period, even up to the early 1920s, although from then until some forty years later, matting was relegated to porches, summer houses and to some year-round houses as an inexpensive, substitute carpet. A far cry from the fashionable mattings George Washington used at Mount Vernon in the 18th century.

Representatives of W. & J. Sloane at a factory in Kobe, Japan, 1905. Note the wide variety of patterned mattings offered. Chinese mattings of the same period were not available in such a wide range.

In the 1970s there has been a revival of matting for year-round use in all parts of the house. Jack Lenor Larsen, an innovative textile designer, began to use coir matting in wide strips or tiles, urethane backed or plain, as a wall-to-wall floor surface for major living areas.

The "natural look" has become "the" look, with soft sand colors and natural materials—wicker, straw, linen, and vegetable-fiber floor coverings of sisal, hemp, rush, coir, and maize. No longer are mattings relegated solely to beach houses, porches, and summer floors; no longer are they shunned as a cheap substitute for carpeting; no longer, indeed, are they inexpensive, ranging in price from $5.95 to about $50.00 per square yard.

Detail of China matting (probably late 19th century) still nailed to the floor in the upstairs bedroom of "The Hermitage," Ho-Ho-Kus, New Jersey, showing fragments of newspapers used as padding.

One of the interesting characteristics of mattings, especially sisal, is their reaction to atmospheric conditions. Too dry and they stretch; too damp and they may ripple; too wet, and they shrink and mildew. Formerly the danger of matting's slipping when laid flat on bare floorboards was counteracted with under-layers of newspapers. Today many of the mattings come with a plastic backing which gives not only dimensional stability but prevents the slipping, shrinking, stretching, and buckling that were formerly a problem. Some contemporary mattings in tiles are from 12 to $19\frac{3}{4}$ inches square, backed with PVC, and as long as these tiles fit tightly within the space allotted for them, no gluing is necessary except at doorways. These same mattings are available by the yard, in rug sizes, flat or pile weaves, plain colors and stripes. Sisal stays the cleanest, has fire-retardant qualities, and is one of the strongest natural fibers, used in ropes for mooring ships as well as floor covering.

Especially for city-dwellers, where the landlord may require it or noise from the neighbors may indicate their use, mattings provide an alternative to wall-to-wall carpeting and an effective soundproofing on walls. With the exception of straw, maize, and Japanese tatami, these mattings are rough-textured and scratchy, but they form a serene floor covering when alone or as a neutral background for area rugs, whether elegant antique, Oriental, Navajo, fur, handcrafted, or the ultimate in contemporary design.

3 From Rags to Riches

Rag scraps were a commodity which, sooner or later, everyone in America possessed. They were a worn-out by-product of garments, bedding, and household furnishings. They were no longer large enough or strong enough to be recut into new garments, reworked into new household textiles, or re-stitched into new quilts. The fabrics represented a valuable commodity none-theless, a textile of flax or wool which had taken considerable energy to obtain or produce. Flax and wool were the two primary raw materials used for textiles in the 18th century. Flax required months from planting until the fibers were spun into thread and woven, while wool, sheared, carded and spun from sheep brought from Europe, was a treasured family possession. The rags, scraps and snippets of these fabrics were carefully saved, salvaged and converted once again—as long strips stitched together, or as small scraps—into meager floor coverings. They were given new strength by new construction. Certainly there were a few woven carpets even in the remote towns in colonial America, which served as a floor-covering model. But most rugs and carpets in those early days were made up from scraps, worked into gaily striped coverings for the floor, parquet or stone, or other, even finer, carpets. Regardless of the construction, these rag floor coverings added warmth to the room, reducing the drafts—a substitute albeit very limited, for the imported woven carpets and mattings which were the prized possessions of a few wealthy families.

"List" was the 18th-century name for the 36-inch-wide carpets using selvedge or evenly cut strips of fabrics left from garment-making or textile-weaving. The rugs were woven with a worsted, wool, cotton or linen warp, and described in the 1807 *Book of Trades or Library of the Useful Arts* as "another sort of carpet in use . . . made of narrow slips of list sewed together; these of course are very inferior to those just described [i.e. Axminster]."[1] Nevertheless, list carpets were important enough in the 18th century to be listed as "a List floor Cloth 7/6" in the 1749 inventory of George Charleton of Williamsburg.[2] They were also advertised for sale during the 1760s in the *Boston Gazette* for use as a stair-covering.

There was European precedent for use of the list carpets in America to cover parquet or stone or as protection for other carpets. In the Netherlands, Tibout Regters painted "The Family of Jacob van Stamhorst" seated at a table placed on a striped carpet, that may well have been a rag carpet.[3] Other list carpets were recorded in European "conversation piece" paintings during the 18th century.

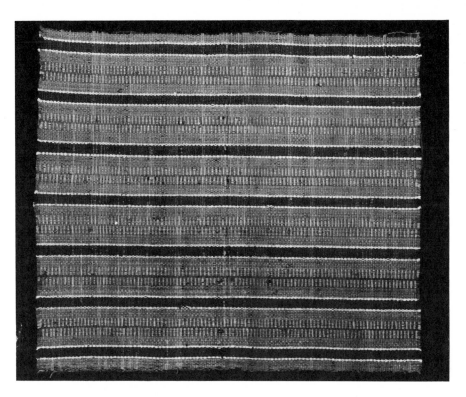

Quaker striped carpet with rag or list weft. Woven in Burlington, New Jersey during the late 18th century by Mercy English.

Even well into the 19th century, however, list carpets, although prevalent, were by no means universal. Samuel Griswold Goodrich wrote early in the century that in Ridgefield, Connecticut "carpets were . . . only known in a few families, and were confined to the keeping-room and parlor. They were all home made: the warp consisted of woolen yarn and the woof of lists and old woolen cloth, cut into strips and sewed together at the ends."[4] Ridgefield was only one of the hundreds of communities where these striped floor coverings were made. In the "best room" of a mid-1830s home in the State of Massachusetts was a "homemade carpet, carefully woven with strips of cloth, in which red, blue and yellow, are nicely adjusted to produce the best effect."[5]

However, the rag carpeting, itself a substitute for finer floor coverings, was not without its own time- or money-saving imitations. An entry in the daily journal of a New Hampshire minister's wife recorded that in two days she had painted her parlor floor "striped with red, green, blue, yellow and purple—carpet like."[6]

Rag carpeting was a practical, durable floor covering. It was reversible and washable, and, as Candace Wheeler recommended later in the 19th century, it could be put outside on the grass, subject to the vagaries of wind, rain and sun.[7] Also, it could be easily swept clean, although the 1884 domestic book entitled *Household Conveniences* made the following admonishment about their care: "Sweep carpets gently. Even a rag carpet should be treated with consideration. A severe digging with a stiff broom wears the warp and scrapes out the lint of the rags quite needlessly."[8] It did have, however, one disadvantage caused by its flexible construction—corners were frequently flipped back, and the surface was frequently rippled.

Rare example of rag carpeting with woven warp stripes and stencil pineapple pattern; probably dating from the first half of the 19th century.

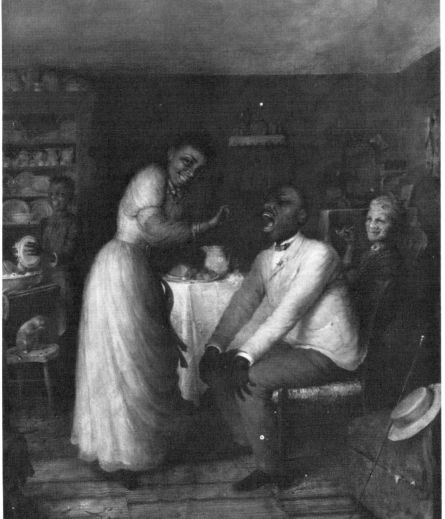

"Blind Faith" painted by Lilly Martin Spencer, *c*. 1890. Typical example of ordinary hit-and-miss rag carpeting woven in strips and seamed together with little regard for matching pattern. Rippling is a problem when flatwoven carpets are not nailed to the floor.

Woven rag carpeting was produced throughout the 19th century at home and in mills. But curiously enough, it was predominantly hand-woven even into the 20th century. E. C. Beetem & Son, who began manufacturing "Colonial Rag Carpets" in Carlisle, Pennsylvania in 1876, used only hand-operated looms until the mill. was finally closed in 1951. Beetem commented "anyone could learn to weave rag carpets in a week or less, and while there were weaving guilds in the cities of highly skilled weavers who were familiar with the most complicated warps and weaves, their weaving was of the simplest order."[9] Most of the rugs were 36 inches wide, but they also had hand-operated broad looms on which 9, 12 or 15 foot wide carpets could be woven in a single piece. Looms on which the wide rugs were woven had such heavy beater bars that two men were usually required to operate them.

Numerous patterns and color combinations were possible in these rag carpets, from simple crosswise stripes in which the colors were governed by the multicolor hit-and-miss rags used in the weft, to sophisticated plaids requiring specially colored and arranged warp, and planned use of random colored or dyed rag weft. Rags used in this commercially produced carpeting could be fastened together with a special stapling machine which reduced the time required for preparing the rugs, but the finest carpets were made with rags lapped and stitched by hand, because the joint was smoother and flatter. Rovings, soft multi-ply ropes of slightly twisted unspun cotton, were also a popular form of filling for the commercial carpets, the use of which began during the Civil War when the women were preparing bandages and knitting instead of sewing rags and winding them into balls for carpets. Roving was a heavy, water-resistant filling, well suited for making carpets.

Beetem also made "Tea Room" carpets—small patterned, hand-woven carpets particularly used in early-20th-century tea rooms. Tea rooms evolved out of a social change brought about by widespread use of the automobile. It caused the gradual demise of railroad and country hotels, with their restaurants serving home-cooked foods, replaced by roadside stands which catered to the automobile trade. In the early 20th century tea rooms, often front rooms of houses, served home-cooked foods in the tradition of country inns. They were simply furnished with mission furniture—square oak tables covered with paper or linen doilies, and straight-backed chairs. Walls were painted in light pastel colors or papered with striped chintz wallpapers. The most stylish of these tea rooms were carpeted in small block or checked patterns, hand-woven in the "craftsman mode." These carpets were usually made with cotton warps, although the finest were made with wool warps and with jute and linen roving filling the thickness of a pencil and requiring about four filling shots per inch. The rovings were dyed blue, green, brown, old rose and yellow to accentuate the warp colors in combinations of violet, black and linen color; mulberry, black and pink; purple, lettuce-green and dark bottle green; in light olive, rose and black. In some tea rooms established by antique dealers, objects were for sale. E. C. Beetem recalled an instance in which "even the rugs and carpetings were sold off the floors and carried off by seekers of hand-made things, who packed them into their cars."[10]

Rag rugs are still available, some with the traditional worn-out rag fillings,

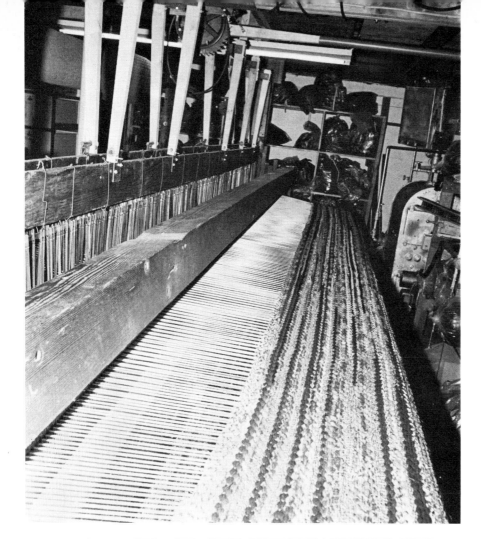

Hand loom built in
Pennsylvania *c.* 1900 for weaving
15-feet-wide rag carpets. Still in
use, it can be operated by a
single weaver.

"Tea Room" carpets hand-
woven with wool or cotton warp
and roving weft at the mill of
E. C. Beetem and Son, Carlisle,
Pennsylvania, during the early
20th century.

Even by the 1860s bare wood floors, with an occasional small braided or woven mat were still more common than carpeted ones.

many with all-new materials. The majority are now commercially woven on power looms, but there are numerous craftsmen producing custom hand-woven rag rugs on the old hand looms, continuing the 18th-century rug form with materials salvaged from textile manufacturing processes, using materials too good to be thrown away, but too fragmentary for many other uses.

There were numerous other methods of manipulating the long strips of rags to create other forms of rag carpeting. Braided mats were another form recorded in 19th-century paintings, engravings and writings. As early as 1827, "A Miss M. Locke, of Andover, Massachusetts was presented with a prize at an agricultural fair for a rug of braided rags, very pretty, $2.00."[11]

Such braided rugs were popular, and practical, using carefully folded strips to produce the smooth, even braids. Two methods of construction evolved: Three or more strand braids were made, then laced to the preceding row with a needle and heavy thread, or the braids were worked into the preceding row to make a continuous flat braided surface. This slightly more difficult method interlacing the new row with the previous one, eliminated the stitching. In either method of construction, great care was required to maintain an even tension on the braids to insure that the rug lay flat when it was finished. A wide variety of shapes could be created by braiding—round, oval, square or rectangular, or combination shapes, used for stairs and halls, as well as door mats and room-sized rugs. Careful selection and proportion of colors can create a wide variety of textures and color gradations.

With the revival of interest in early American handicrafts shortly after the turn of the 20th century, rug braiding gained renewed popularity. "Braid aids," small metal cones using the principle of a binding foot attachment on a sewing machine, were introduced during the 1930s to speed up the process of folding the strips before braiding. One such aid was needed for each strand of fabric.

Braiding was taught through arts-and-crafts leagues, especially in the New

England area; it became part of W.P.A. projects and was taught by television demonstration in the early 1950s. Large braided rugs were especially popular during the 1940s and 1950s for the "thousands of new homes which are springing up all over the country."[12]

For those with neither time for nor interest in home manufacture, Sears, Roebuck & Company in 1927 advertised braided yarn rugs in the manner of braided rag ones in hit-or-miss patterns, with pink or blue borders; a 3 feet by 4 feet rug for $3.98. "Quaint and attractive, oval rag rugs of popular old fashioned design." Hit-or-miss pattern, washable, reversible, rag rugs were available for between 89 cents and $4.50, depending on size.

In 1974 braided rugs of fabric and yarn were still offered for sale by Sears, Roebuck—flat-braided "Colonial rugs" in variations of orange, blue, gold, green, brown, or hit-and-miss multicolor. Many of the braided rugs now available are braided by hand or machine, but instead of being laced together with invisible stitches, protected from wear by the folds of the braids, they are stitched together with machine zig-zagging. Even with the widespread commercial production of braided rugs, however, many are still braided by hand, in colors and patterns reflecting the ambitions and talents of the maker.

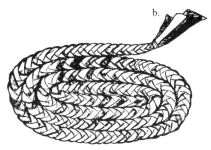

Simple method of construction of an oval braided rug. a. First step in preparing to lace braids together. b. Continuous braided strand laced together to form the center of rug.

"The Rug Braider" painted by Della Garretson, 1932. Working flat on a table, the worker is lacing the braid to the finished section of rug.

Left above:
Hit and miss crochet rug,
probably early 20th century.

Right:
Details of garter stitch, ridge
stitch and lacing on Berks
County rug.

Left below:
Rug from Berks County,
Pennsylvania, with wool-
embroidered center,
surrounded by rows of ridge-
stitch crochet. The outer bands
are made of knitted garter stitch
sewed to the crochet.

Opposite:
"Chief Justice and Mrs. Oliver
Ellsworth" painted by Ralph Earl
in 1792 shows a kind of floor
covering which could have been
painted, flatwoven or woven in
some other way. The patterning
of this floor covering and that of
a similar one in the portrait
"Mrs. Noah Smith and her
Children," also painted by
Ralph Earl and now in the
Metropolitan Museum of Art,
New York, suggests ingrain
carpeting.

Overleaf:
Natural fiber mattings available
in America today. Like those of
the 18th and 19th centuries they
are imported. *Top row, left to
right:* hand-woven maize square
from China; rush and straw
"Circle in a Square" from
China; two-tone flatwoven sisal.
Middle row, left to right: natural
cocoa fiber, with two-color
stripe; bulky woven sisal;
flatwoven Coir. *Bottom row, left
to right:* loop-pile cocoa bristle,
vinyl backed, available as tiles or
by the yard; brush-pile sisal,
vinyl backed.

Both knitted and crocheted rugs also make use of the long strips of fabric. Both make frugal use of scraps, of strips cut and stitched end to end. As with all other rag rugs, preparation of the rags to a large extent determined the final patterns. By using a total random color selection, a hit-and-miss round, oval or rectangular rug would result, which, with consistent, even tension, would lie flat on the floor. Once finished, the rug was reversible and washable. Sometimes crochet was combined with knitting, or with knitting and embroidery to create a decorative rug, such as the one illustrated, from Berks County, Pennsylvania. With the revival of handcrafts in the 1970s, crochet rugs have become a new fashion. Most of the crochet rugs, adaptations of the granny square bed coverings, and open, lacy shawl patterns, are now made with yarns, instead of rag strips. Much softer than many of the old rag varieties, they require padding or double-face tape to prevent them from sliding on the floor.

"Knitted rugs have much to recommend them," wrote Candace Wheeler in 1900. "They can be made of all sorts of pieces, even the smallest; they wear well, and can easily be made beautiful."[13] Traditionally they have been both of rags and yarns, in entirely knitted rugs, or in combination with other construction techniques. Most knitted rugs are worked in narrow strips. Some are made in rectangles, stitched together in log-cabin-type patterns, then stitched to a backing for additional stability, such as one at the Henry Ford Museum. Others are made in a continuous strip, and wound spiral fashion, each row stitched to the one before.

A variation of the knitted strip rug was introduced in *Godey's Lady's Book* in the 1860s, and later instructions were included in *What Every One Should Know*, a domestic handbook of 1888. Using strips of woolen or flannel cloth, 3 inches long and half an inch wide, they "were a good way to use up discarded coats, vests and pants . . . broadcloth, waterproof, ladies' cloth, etc. [and

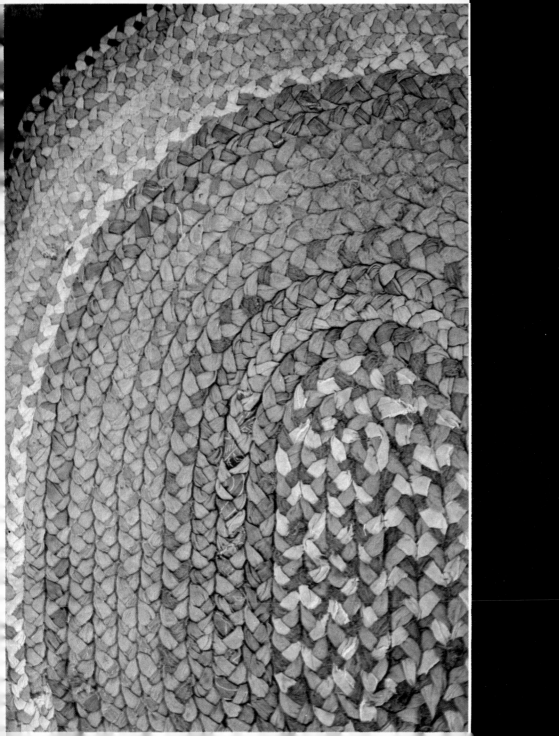

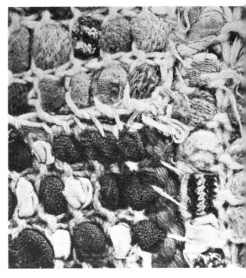

remnants of string were] the best for the purpose." These rugs were particularly desirable and suitable for doorways. They were constructed in strips, with strips of fabric knitted into the string base to form a shaggy, tufted surface. Strips were then stitched together with an over-and-over stitch. Although the instructions for the shaggy rug recommended use of new jute twine, "the same that is used in making gunny-sacks," not all were made with it. Many used whatever pieces of string—red, blue, white, or brown—were available.[14] One, with instructions and in progress, is part of the Smithsonian Institution collection; another with the date 1885 worked into the center is at the Shelburne Museum. Some, unnoticed late-19th and early-20th-century examples, encrusted with mud and grime, still grace doorways.

As the vogue for hearth rugs increased during the last years of the 18th century and the first decades of the 19th, new ways were devised to make these rugs from local and leftover materials. The industrial revolution with its machines for faster spinning, weaving, and processing of raw materials, and the subsequent growth of the American textile industry, had gradually made factory woven fabrics available. But even these materials—carefully saved by thrifty housewives—in turn became scraps or rags, to be converted by new techniques into pile mats and rugs.

Some of the earliest of these pile-surface rag rugs were the shirred rugs—caterpillar, button and bias—inventive constructions popular from about the 1820s to the 1850s. All were variations on a construction theme. Scraps of fabric were stitched to the backing, so closely packed that they had to remain upright, forming a dense pile surface.[15]

In all of them the surface fabrics were stitched on to a homespun backing to form a dense, pile surface. Because the stitches were exposed, it was a fragile construction. Bias shirred rugs could be made either with straight grain or bias strips, folded in half along the length of the strips. The folded edge was stitched to the backing according to the pattern; the raw edges formed the pile. Fine linear detailing, careful gradations of color, and a wavy line quality are characteristics of these rugs.

Above left:
Black-bordered shaggy or fluff mat made with small strips of fabric and dated 1885.

Above right:
Detail of a shaggy mat showing the use of different fabrics in the pile, miscellaneous pieces of string for knitted base, and the method of joining strips.

Overleaf:
"The Sheldon House" in Deerfield, Massachusetts, was worked in a straight-grain shirred technique on linen by Mrs Arabella Sheldon Wells in 1844. This rug and a companion piece are two of the earliest signed and dated examples of this technique.

Opposite:
Detail of a rug braided by Candace Wheeler during the late 19th century incorporating patterned fabrics designed by the Associated Artists. The color scheme and pattern reflects her concern for the proper "arrangement of colour."

Various types of shirring.
a. Pleated shirring.
b. "Caterpillar" shirring. c. Bias
shirring.

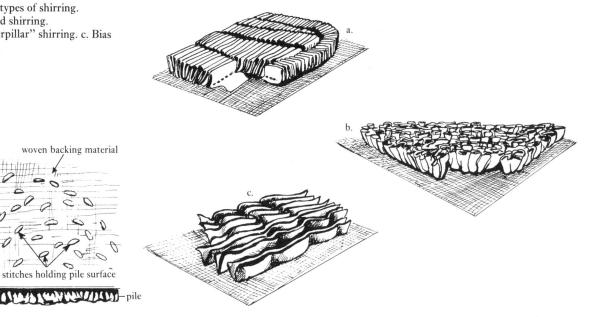

a.

b.

c.

woven backing material

stitches holding pile surface

pile

Reverse of a shirred rug
showing stitches.

Detail of an appliquéd rug in the
collection of the Henry Ford
Museum, Dearborn, Michigan.
Each petal is carefully secured
and bordered by buttonhole
stitches.

In pleated shirred rugs, long strips of fabric were pleated accordion fashion and stitched to the background. The method, providing wide stripes of uncut pile surface, was well adapted to large, solid-colored background areas, but was usually used in combination with chenille shirring if intricate pattern detailing, such as leaves or flowers, was necessary. Chenille, or caterpillar shirring, permitted considerable detailing and produced a dense pile surface closely resembling hooked rugs. Strips of fabric were folded lengthwise, then stitched along the cut edges—producing an uncut pile—or along the folded edges, producing a cut pile. This latter form, often surrounded with a braided border, seems to be a typically Shaker innovation. The strips were then gathered along the thread into "caterpillars" and stitched on to the backing. Floral, geometric, and many other patterns were created in this manner. And there were variations to this technique as well. On one New England hearth rug of the 19th century, caterpillar shirring was used only for the pattern flowers in reds, pinks and blues, and for the leaves in green. The dark broadcloth on which the caterpillars were sewn provided the plain background.

Button rugs, which could use even smaller scraps of fabrics, were pile rugs made of tiny circles of fabric, folded in quarters, and stitched at the apex to the backing. The placement was usually so close that the circles stayed folded and formed a dense, resilient pile—often impossible to distinguish from hooked rugs without looking for the stitches on the back side.

The pile-surface button rug had a flat-surface, appliquéd counterpart sometimes known as a button rug, but more commonly as a dollar mat. These mats were not a substantial floor-covering, but provided a decorative hearth-rug. Broadcloth or felted-wool circles of various sizes and colors were cut out. Like three coins of decreasing size, they were stitched with buttonhole or overcast stitches, one on top of the next, each stack then stitched on to a backing—ticking, wool or homespun. At the Henry Ford Museum, one of the most

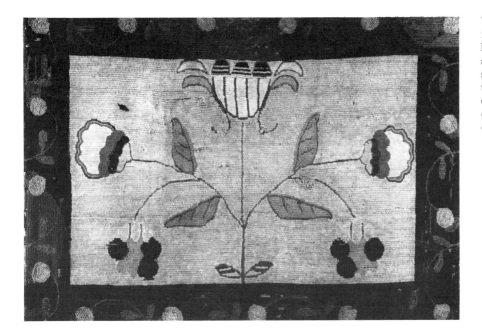

This rug was hooked on linen from which warp and weft yarns had been removed, thus forming a grid through which the fabric strips would pass. It is believed to be one of the earliest examples of an American hooked rug dating from the early 19th century.

spectacular of the dollar rugs, probably of late-19th-century Shaker origin, combines the diamond pattern arrangement of dollars in combinations of red, black and indigo blue, with hit-and-miss hooking, and a blue, brown and white braided border. Another example with overlapping petals of flowers, secured with button hole stitches to the background, provided a colorful decorative alternative.

Widespread use of carpeting, wall-to-wall and as hearth and door rugs, became an increasingly important decorative element in America towards the end of the first half of the 19th century. For those who could afford it, there were both American and English carpetings available. Textile mills produced vast quantities of cotton and woolen fabrics, providing dress and household fabrics in greater and greater abundance, the rags and scraps of which continued to be saved for other uses. But perhaps one of the greatest influences in American floor-covering history, both for home and mill production, was the increased importation of Asiatic jute. This fiber, woven into burlap fabric, was widely used as a wrapping for raw commodities such as cotton, and for grain and feed sacks. It was sturdy, available and adaptable. This coarse fabric, when opened at the seams, provided a backing of a size suitable for a hearth rug. The burlap was coarse enough to allow narrow strips of rags to be pulled through the burlap from the back using a hook, such as a crochet or button hook, to make a pile surface carpet; yet the fabric was fine enough to permit hooking an unending array of detailed patterns. The hooked rug, a form developing after the 1840s, became a widespread American form, again transforming waste materials into a useful and beautiful object. It was a form which enabled the fashionable woven carpet patterns to be translated into an effective substitute and one which gave the worker's fancy and imagination free rein.

Patterns on the hooked rugs encompassed everything—from geometrics which resembled patterns of floorcloths, flower baskets and favorite animals to oriental rug motifs and assorted combinations. The quality of the finished product depended on the skill of the worker. Some of the patterns were undoubtedly copies from existing rugs, some drawn by professional itinerant painters, some drawn by the worker herself. To hook a large rug was a great enterprise which required considerable planning. For a room-size 19th-century floral example "Mother evolved the design herself, painting it on the floor of an upstairs bedroom to see if it was satisfactory. It took her two years to hook the carpet, still in grand condition, but the floor she painted is now covered with new boards . . ."[16] Besides drawing the pattern directly on the fabric, printing blocks—similar to those used for embroidery—were used to print the pattern on burlap. Chambers and Lealand, a Massachusetts company, which made copper-inlaid wooden stamping blocks during the 1860s, sold the blocks to Philena Moxley, an embroideress who used them for printing rug patterns.

Stenciling patterns on to burlap was an adaptation of the procedure used for decades by the itinerant painters and floorcloth manufacturers. It was a method successfully adapted by Edward Sands Frost, a Yankee peddlar, to hooked-rug patterns. In 1868, while living in Biddeford, Maine, his wife began to hook a

"Lion and Palm" adapted from the Edward Frost pattern, "Lion pattern No. 7," *c.* 1880. Numerous variations on this theme are known.

"Lion Pattern No. 7" was one of the beloved and frequently copied or adapted patterns created by E. S. Frost.

LION PATTERN, No. 7.

PRICE 90 Cents.   Size 7-8 x 1 3-4 Yds.

rug. ". . . I noticed that she was using a very poor hook," he later recollected, "so being a machinist, I went to work and made the crooked hook . . . which is still in vogue today."[17]

Frost became so enamored with his wife's project that he helped finish the first rug. He decided that he could make a better pattern, and designed one with flowers and scrolls. Neighbors, seeing the new pattern, began to order some like it, and soon the demand was so great that he could no longer supply the patterned rug-backings. "Yankee-like" he began "to study some way to do them quicker. Then the first idea of stencilling presented itself to me."[18] Using old tin and copper wash kettles, he made his own tools and punches for cutting stencils out of the metal. Each of the various design elements, flowers, scrolls, leaves, had its own stencil, which he combined in various ways on the rug backing. He peddled these rug designs, which became increasingly popular, from his cart. Soon he was revamping his individual pattern elements into 36 inch by 72 inch rug sizes. Only two years later, Frost, the rug man, had devised a method of printing his rug patterns in color, "so as to sell them at a profit."

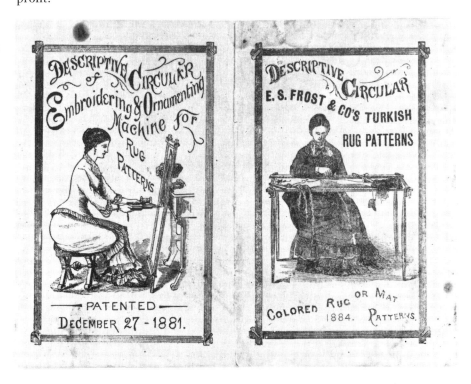

Front and back covers of Frost's catalogue of 1884 showing two methods of making hooked rugs, one of which included use of a new "machine" to speed up the process.

Within a few years, poor health forced Frost to sell his business, which was continued in Biddeford, Maine until 1900—by then the accessibility of inexpensive machine-made rugs had diminished the popularity of hooked rugs. But the story does not end there. In the 1930s, Mrs. Charlotte Stratton, an ardent and accomplished New England rug hooker, discovered the stencil plates, which had been sold to a Lowell, Massachusetts belt-manufacturer. She bought the stencils, and used them as teaching aids for her students, sharing them with others interested in rug-hooking. She encouraged the revival of the

Ebenezer Ross of Toledo, Ohio,
developed a rug "machine," now
known as a shuttle hook. It was
sold, along with his patterns,
during the last years of the 19th
century.

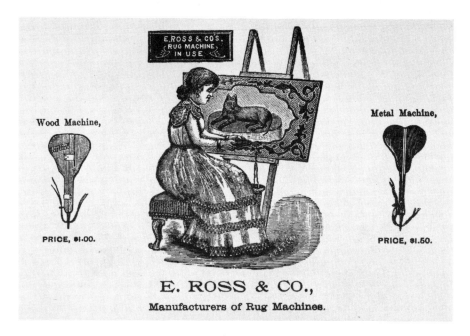

Hooked rug with Oriental
pattern which, since it could be
made at home, enabled many
households to have a fancy,
fashionable rug in their parlor.

craft, which during the 1920s and 1930s was in vogue. Now the entire collection of Frost stencils is in the collection of the Greenfield Village, Henry Ford Museum, in Dearborn, Michigan. The nearly 750 different stencils which could be used to produce roughly 180 designs are still being used to produce rug patterns in anything from three to eighteen colors. Several of the original rugs, made from the Frost stencils, are also in that collection.

Other popular late-19th-century hooked-rug patterns are attributed to Ebenezer Ross, who had devised a new "Novelty Rug Machine" available in both wood and metal models, a device to make rug-hooking faster. This was the earliest of the punch-hooks, adapted to use either narrow-cut rags or carpet yarns. Ross, established in Toledo, Ohio, sold patterns and rug yarns as well, to

Oriental rug patterns offered by E. S. Frost in 1881.

help promote his new rug machine. His first catalogue included fifty-six colored prints, many of them copies of the popular patterns by Frost.[19]

In the early 20th century, the old craft of rug-hooking became a fairly widespread cottage industry throughout the Eastern United States and Canada. The skills were there, the market for Early American was there, encouraged by numerous large hooked-rug auctions, and there was a need for additional income. Major Canadian centers included the Grenfell Mission of Labrador, Cape Breton and Nova Scotia, where the Cheticamp hooked-rug industry was established and, according to the *Christian Science Monitor* in 1939, was "catering to New York decorators who order rugs to be used in palatial homes."[20]

One of the earliest hooked-rug industries in America was founded in 1902

Some tools for making hooked
rugs. a. Shuttle hooker;
mid-20th century. b. Adjustable
punch needle; early 20th
century. c. Automatic hook rug
needle; *c.* 1920.

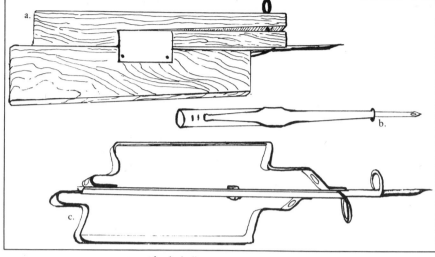

Cross-section of looped and
cut-pile hooked rug construction.
The rug hook is passed through
the backing fabric and pulls up
the pile yarns or strips held
underneath through the same
hole to the surface.

Two types of rug hooks currently
available. a. With a bent shank.
b. More usual type with a
straight shank.

by Lucy Thomson of Belchertown, Massachusetts, who specialized in
American Indian motifs, as did the New Hampshire community founded by
Helen Albee, which produced the Abnakee hooked rugs.[21]

In these communities, as well as in similar ones in Boston, Maine, Tennessee,
North Carolina, Kentucky and Virginia, each worker made the entire product
at home, then either sold it through a community organization, a roadside
stand such as those still seen in West Virginia and other southern states, or
directly from her home. "We have nothing that savors of factory work," wrote
Mrs. F. D. Huckabee, who was teaching Tennessee mountain women to make
hooked rugs. "Each piece is made in the home of the worker."[22]

After World War I, the home craft of rug-hooking began to find a new direction when two British immigrants, Mr. and Mrs. Alfred Porter, took positions
as domestic servants in one of the great country houses on Long Island. Once,
to pass the time during one of their employer's frequent, prolonged absences,
they made a hooked rug. Alfred drew the pattern on an old bath towel, and his
wife hooked it in the old American way. By now the story may be legend, but
their crude, home made rug was part of the emergence of a whole new industry
—that of custom design, hand-crafted rugs. But that is another chapter.

However, interest in rug-hooking as a home craft waned until the 1960s
when it revived once again—this time as a creative artistic outlet based on the
traditional forms. Rug-making was part of a larger handcraft revival, one which
practiced the old forms of handcraft as well as contemporary interpretations
combining the use of traditional tools and materials in new textures and
patterns.

The idea of thoughtful, frugal use of available materials, and their conversion into high quality products, was epitomized for nearly a century by the Shakers. The products of this unique religious group were sought after by the people of the "outside world." Living in isolated communities—the first of which, Watervliet, near Albany, New York, was founded in 1774 by Ann Lee—the Shakers and their communities multiplied until, by 1826, there were 18 established, self-sufficient communes. The Shakers, like many other settlers, raised flax for their textiles and sheep to provide wool for extensive flannel and knitted underwear industries. Long known for cleanliness, they also began cultivating broom corn for making brooms during the last decades of the 18th century. By 1817 they could no longer produce sufficient raw materials for their industry—since a single person could make 2,500 brooms between fall and spring, and had to purchase broom corn from the outside. Many of their wares were sold to merchants in surrounding towns. One of the brethren, Theodore Bates, invented the flat broom, an item still in common use today, and as rugs became fashionable toward the end of the 19th century, the Shakers began to manufacture carpet-beaters and rug-whips.

All property in the Shaker communities was communal, most of it produced by hand, and the work, thought and effort which was required to produce these articles was widely respected within the community and from the outside.

The Shaker communities abided by the Millennial Laws of 1821, a secret code revised in 1845 which governed every aspect of their lives.[23] Its rulings

Corner of Shaker rag rug showing characteristic rags and twisted yarns arranged in stripes, multiple borders in three (or more) strands, and narrow hand-woven tape.

Ravel knit rug, of late 19th or
early 20th century; believed to
be Shaker. These rugs always
have linear, geometric patterns.

Strips of ravel knit goods
stitched to a backing of ingrain
carpeting.

formalized the respect for property, and determined in minute detail not only
much of the interior furnishings, but also its care. "When brethren and sisters
go up and down stairs, they should not slip their feet on the carpet, or floor,
but lift them up and set them down plumb, so as not to wear out the carpets or
floor unnecessarily. Also when they turn at the head or foot of the stairs, they
should not turn their feet on the floor, lest they wear holes in it." The Millennial
laws also directed that "The carpets in one room should be as near alike as can
consistently be provided, and these the deaconnesses should provide."[24]
Other Shaker writings recorded an inspirational message received by one of the
sisters in 1841—an early attempt to regulate the possessions in the retiring or
dwelling rooms. Specific mention was made regarding the patterning of carpets.
"Carpets are admissible, but they ought to be used with discretion, and made
plain. Mother Lucy says two colors are sufficient for one carpet. Make one strip
of red and green, another of drab and gray, another of butternut and gray.

The binding yarn may also be of two colours, and also the binding if necessary . . ."[25] These rugs were probably the plain, woven carpets using a rag or combination rag-and-wool weft, in which two colors of weft are twisted to give a barber-pole effect, and combined in subtle variations and plain colors to make stripes. Although the weaving was primarily the work of the sisters, who entered "Linen for Stair carpets," "90 yards of rag carpeting," "stair cloths"

and "flag carpets" in their yearly accounts of weaving,[26] Benjamin Gates, a Shaker tailor, mentioned that he cut carpet rags along with picking apples and printing seed bills.[27]

Ravel-knit rugs, characterized by a long shaggy pile, with the texture of unraveled knitted goods, are also believed to be a 19th-century Shaker floor covering, although no examples remain in the Shaker villages. Usually, the simple geometric patterns—stripes, diamonds or squares—are created with reds, browns, blue, and a fine black-and-white stripe. The knitted underwear industry, in which the Shakers were engaged, may have provided the scraps for these rugs.

Elaborate patterned knitted rugs, and a number of hooked rugs, with braided outer borders, making thrifty use of scraps, added warmth and color to the austere Shaker dwellings.

Practical floor coverings such as braided, rag and fluff rugs were made in the

Elaborate Shaker knitted rug in which the center ring was formed by stitching one long band together snail-fashion. The ends of the outer bands are carefully butted together.

communities and sold through the community stores. Plush rugs, a fancier type, were advertised in an 1870s Shaker catalogue. They sold at 75 cents per square foot, and were available in white, yellow, maroon, blue-black or old gold. They could be made to any dimension with footstools and pillows to match. However, although the Shakers made floor coverings which were also sold in their stores or through their catalogues, production was intended first to supply the needs of the community. This same philosophy—which changed somewhat during the 20th century—was also true for most of the domestic 19th-century rag rugs which, by clever adaptation of materials at hand, fulfilled a household need for something pretty, bright and useful.

Button-shirred, banded rug with horse motif and multiple braid edging from Shakertown at Pleasant Hill, Kentucky; late 19th century.

4 Floorcloths, Oilcloths and Linoleums

For more than two centuries floorcloths, oilcloths and painted canvases have been used as substitutes for carpets in hallways and on stairs, and as floor coverings in their own right. They were documented by pattern, material and areas of use as early as 1728, when "Two old checquered canvas' to lay under a table" and a "large painted Canvas Square as the Room" were appraised at the substantial sum of £8 in the inventory of Governor William Burnet of Massachusetts.[1] This entry suggests that carpet substitutes were found in the homes of the wealthy.

A stern warning appeared in the *Encyclopaedia of Architecture* in 1739 that "nothing is more injurious to the floors than covering them with painted floor cloth, which entirely prevents the access of atmospheric air, whence the dampness of the boards never evaporates, and it is well known that oak and fir posts have been brought into premature decay."[2] Yet it was this very impervious quality which made these substitutes so suitable for "...Rooms, Passages and Stairs."[3] Mud and moisture could be easily mopped up and floorcloth could be "Repainted and Ornamented in the best manner"[4] either at home or at the upholsterers'.

Floorcloths were part of a long search for other substitute materials with qualities which were sought—materials which were "impervious to air" and easy to care for, and could be "painted at home or sent to the upholsterers," and still look as though they belonged in the inventory of Governor Burnet of Massachusetts. Floorcloths, oilcloths and linoleums were all carpetings that reflected the patterns of the industrial growth and the culture of America.

In the 1750s the English precedent for the protective covering was acidly commented on by Samuel Johnson, following a visit to a London residence. "On the floor where we sat lay a carpet covered with a cloth of which Prospero ordered his servant to lift up a corner that I might contemplate the brightness of the colours and the elegance of the texture, and asked me whether I had ever seen anything so fine before. I did not gratify his folly with any outcries of admiration, but coldly bade the footman let down the cloth."[5]

In the 18th century floorcloth was a generic term for a substitute carpet of treated or untreated wool, linen, or cotton materials, many of which were used as carpeting. Untreated floorcloths in linen, baize, serge, or drugget—usually plain, but sometimes patterned, as are two in the collection at Williamsburg, one with a salmon-and-blue diamond pattern, the other a small printed geometric in blue, coral, brick and white—were often used in the 18th century

One of many bills for floor coverings purchased by John Cadwalader of Philadelphia. Because the Non-importation Agreement was in effect at that time, it is more than likely that his floorcloths were American made.

Opposite:
"The Tea Party" by Henry Sargent; early 19th century. While there may indeed be a central medallion in this carpet, it is more likely that the large central pattern indicates a separate protective floorcloth.

as a protective covering for fine carpets. Druggets, made in Braintree, Essex and Wilton, Wiltshire, both in England, were a coarse woolen stuff, sometimes available in bright colors and used as floor coverings for room or hall. Those from Essex were reputedly woven into striped and checkered patterns formed by differently colored warp and weft threads. Others were available with printed patterns.[6] Milled drugget, "painted in rich colours" and introduced, according to the *American Family Encyclopaedia,* between 1840 and 1858, was recommended as a "very good substitute for carpets in small apartments."[7]

Baize, also used for floorcloths, was another "sort of open woollen stuff, having a long nap, sometimes frized, and sometimes not," according to *The Cabinet Dictionary* of Thomas Sheraton, published in London.[8]

Family records of John Cadwalader, a member of an old Pennsylvania family, mention that English serge covers were purchased in 1771 in order to protect their best blue Wilton carpet.[9] Aaron Burr of New York, the maverick of early American politics, in the 1790s had a green-bordered "carpet of blue bays to cover the Turkey (ditto) carpet." He used another baize carpet in his dining-room, a green one to protect the Brussels carpeting.[10]

Floorcloths of various sorts were frequently used in dining rooms. "To make sweeping an easy task," a 19th-century household encyclopedia recommended, "get carpets of a kind that are easily swept, then save them from unnecessary litter. Eating should be done in rooms easily cleaned, with carpets of oil-cloth, or similar material, or with bare floors, or with a linen crumb-cloth

Eighteenth-century equipment
for making and stenciling
floorcloths, owned by Joseph
Barnes, London.

One of Barnes' earliest patterns
for floorcloth.

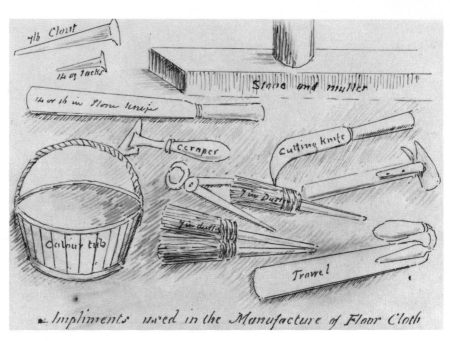

Imploments used in the Manufacture of Floor Cloth

Opposite, top:
Hearth rug *c.* 1840 with an
unusual elephant motif in bias
shirring and a cut-pile, yarn-
sewn embroidered border. The
wavy lines, apparent in center
section, are characteristic of
bias-shirred rugs.

Opposite, bottom:
Pictorial rug, entirely hooked in
yarns portraying popular
storybook characters of the 1930s.

spread upon the carpet underneath the table."[11]

The continuous search for materials—inexpensive, adaptable, pretty—as
alternate and substitute floor coverings, continued. Wallpaper, another available commodity, has also been periodically used as floor covering. In Baltimore,
in 1812, Francis Guy introduced wallpaper carpeting—reputed to be as durable
as canvas floorcloth, but even more beautiful, at about half the price. This carpeting, intended to be used primarily in summer, had been specified as early as
1806.[12] And in 1844 a household book recommended that in order not to waste
old wallpaper scraps, they could be made into a brightly patterned floor
covering, painted with varnish to protect the surface.

Even in 1976, a New Jersey house restorer, a Mr. Weir, was using wallpaper
glued to the floors to provide a permanent decorative surface, which was then
protected by several layers of transparent polyurethane varnish.

Oilcloth was a floorcloth of hemp, linen or cotton treated with an evaporating
oil and paint to make them waterproof. As early as the 1760s a recipe "How to
Make Oil Cloth" for making floor oilcloth was entered in the account book of
Braverter Gray. "Take a drying oil, set it over the fire and then desolve rison
in it (or better gum Lac), there must be so much of either as will bring the
consistency of a balsom. Then add any colour to it you choose."[13]

The "colours" came in an astonishing range, and by the mid-18th century
included green, "chocolate color," red, and plain yellow.[14] Patterns were
produced by a variety of methods: stencils, freehand painting and even
"Carpet printing," as John Gove of Boston advertised, "done in the best and
cheapest manner."[15] Others were decorated in "Straw work and Borders,"
Wilton, and "Turkey Fatcheon" (fashion), printed borders, yellow and black
diamonds, and imitation marble for those who did not want the care of marble
blocks or tile floors, or perhaps the expense.[16] The advantage was that both the
floorcloths and oilcloths could be printed, stenciled or painted. Today it is

difficult to tell one from another because the terms have fallen from common usage and the visual evidence from period paintings could be almost any form. And even the profusely written evidence does not always spell out specific constructions. The 1739 copperplate patterns of John Carwitham[17] and the 1825 instructions of Rufus Porter for stenciling were as applicable to floorcloths as to painted floors.

Many of the treated floorcloths required shipping to reach their destination.

Tools used in linoleum installation today: a. roller. b. hammer. c. compass. d. scissors. e. folding ruler. f. measuring tape. g. plane. h. cutting knife. i. square. j. scraper. k. string. l. brush. m. adhesive container.

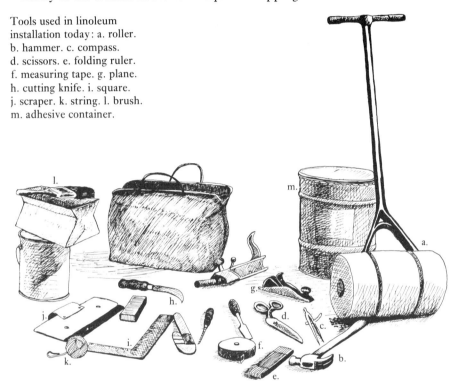

Some were of giant size, rolled to be transported to prevent cracking, but if the merchandise was damaged, the purchaser had a right to complain, as Thomas Nelson of Yorktown did to his London agent: "The Clothe is injur'd by being role'd before the paint was dry."[18] One wealthy southern gentleman gave minute advice about selection, packing and shipping of his order: "one best painted black and white Floor Cloth 16 feet and 6½ long, and 14 feet broad— If they will stow on well, and it is a safe Package—let the Carpet and the floor cloth come over on a Rowler, or Rowlers—." It was also recommended that a thin woolen blanket be put between the layers to prevent the paint from rubbing off.[19]

Though floorcloths continued to be used throughout the 19th century, by 1875 they were commonly referred to as floor oilcloths. A special loom devised in Scotland in the early 19th century permitted the construction of a seamless backing-fabric 24 feet wide. Michael Nairn, later to be involved with producing the first linoleum in America, began weaving floorcloth canvas in Scotland in 1828. By 1847, he manufactured floorcloths. His enterprise was known as "Nairn's Folly" by skeptical townspeople. The invention of Lyalls Positive

Opposite:
Detail of a hooked rug stair covering, 1875. Each tread was worked in a variation of this pattern.

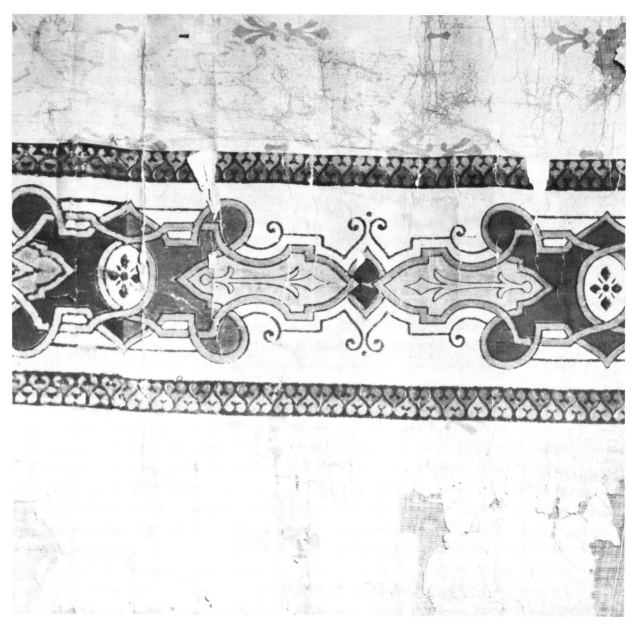

Above and opposite top:
Lightweight bordered
19th-century floor oilcloths,
probably intended for use on
stairs or in halls as protective
coverings over carpet or good
floors.

Motion Loom in America made possible rapid production of these excessively
wide goods. They were made by the Planet Mills in Brooklyn, where they
became special commodity items. After a devastating fire in 1875, the factory
was rebuilt, with 25 canvas looms, and carpet looms as well.

Coarse jute or flax was used in weaving the canvas backing, although flax was
preferred because it was strong and more absorbent of the paint and oils than
hemp was, forming a stronger bond. Lengths of this fabric, 25 to 30 yards long
and 8 yards wide, would be tightly stretched on a vertical frame. Both surfaces
were then covered with hot size or starch to stiffen and seal the fabric. Once
thoroughly dry, the entire surface was rubbed smooth with flat pieces of
pumice stone. Then the first coat of paint was applied to both sides. Since the

Simple, geometric 19th-century
floorcloth pattern printed on
coarse burlap resembles carpet
both in pattern and texture.

Lyall's Positive Motion Power looms first exhibited at the Centennial Exposition in Philadelphia made possible the weaving of fabric "8 yards wide and 40 yards long in ten hours, 320 square yards of cloth in a single day." They were suitable for oilcloth foundations and striped, heavy jute carpet.

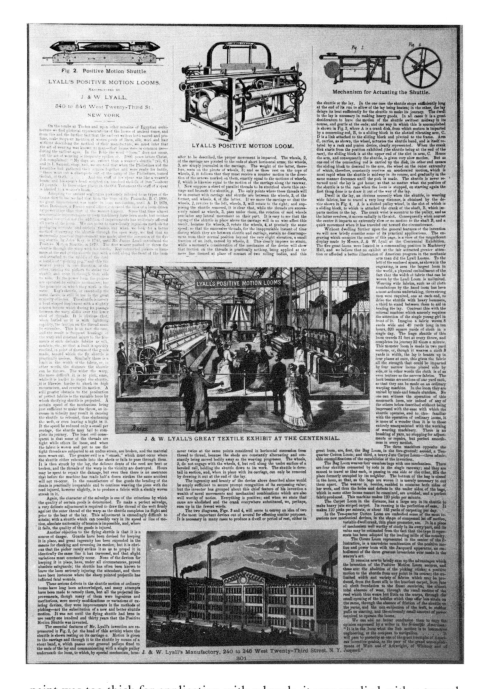

paint was too thick for application with a brush, it was applied with a trowel, much as plaster is. After drying several days, the painted surfaces were smoothed with pumice. This process was repeated four to nine times until the final coat, of thinner, higher-quality paint was applied with a brush. At this point, the floorcloth, weighing 2 to 5 pounds per square yard, resembled a flexible, well-tanned leather hide. The side of the floorcloth to be decorated was again sanded, and those cloths of premium quality were sanded and painted yet again. Patterns in oil colors were frequently applied with 8 to 24 inch square

Wooden block with inset metal designs used for printing floorcloths and early felt-base substitutes for linoleum.

maple wood printing blocks. Numerous blocks were required for a complicated or multicolor pattern—a different block for each color or design element. Patterns were applied from selvage to selvage, printed with all the colors required for the pattern. It was possible for a skilled worker to stamp up to 150 yards per day. On narrow widths, intended for stair and hall coverings, the pattern could be machine printed. Once the entire process was completed, the surface was varnished and dried thoroughly before rolling for shipping.[20]

In 1895 Montgomery Ward offered floorcloths made of a mixture of mineral earth and oil applied to jute cloth; in colors somber or bright, which were printed in small, medium and long patterns, light or dark as desired. The narrow stair-width, inexpensive variety cost 20 cents per square yard, the comparable best quality 36 cents.

These floorcloths made a sturdy, economical floor covering. They did, however, require a certain amount of care as various 19th-century recipes attest. One recommended using the suds left over from the laundry, especially where ammonia had been used, to rub over the surface. Another begins with the dire warning, "To RUIN them, clean them with hot water or soap suds, and leave them half wiped, and they will look very bright while wet, but very dingy and dirty when dry, and will soon crack and peel off. But if you wish to *preserve* them and have them look new and nice, wash them with soft flannels and lukewarm water, and wipe perfectly dry. If you want them to look extra nice, after they are dry, drop a few spoonfuls of milk over them, and rub with a dry cloth."[21]

As late as 1909, when the emphasis was switching to linoleum and felt-based rugs, Sears, Roebuck and Company still offered two multi-colored, geometric-patterned floor oilcloths. Still offered, too, were floor oilcloth stove squares or stove rugs, a patterned oilcloth rug, one and one half to two yards square, designed with a small-patterned geometric center, and a "Turkish" adaptation border. They were available in an assortment of "neat Patterns" usually having a "tan background with harmonizing colors." As the name implies, these small rugs were placed in front of the stove where an excess of wear and cooking spills would occur, protecting the floor or linoleum beneath.[22]

The developing fashion for rugs instead of carpets during the last quarter of the 19th century brought a new emphasis to the wood borders of the floor. Since many houses were not graced with exquisite inlaid parquet, or even hardwood floors, inexpensive imitations were devised to meet the fashion. Floor oilcloth became available in parquet, inlaid, mosaic and oak planking patterns, to fill the space between the wall and rug with pseudo-elegance. With the advent of linoleum, subsequent developments of materials and shifts of fashion, floorcloths and oilcloth floor covering disappeared from the American scene.

Linoleum was developed from the mid-19th-century floorcloths. These were an easy to care for, inexpensive floor covering, but, in the age of new inventions, an improved floorcloth was sought. Numerous experiments with different materials failed: shredded natural sponge and, later, coconut fibers saturated with cement. Finally, in 1844, Elijah Galloway discovered that Indiarubber softened with steam and mixed with granulated cork could be rolled to any thickness through pairs of smooth cast-iron rollers. Extremely expensive, this material, known as Kamptulicon, was available only to public institutions and very wealthy individuals.

The subsequent invention of linoleum in 1863 by the English Indiarubber manufacturer Frederick Walton began a new trend in floor coverings. His invention prompted by the search for an inexpensive substitute for Kamptulicon, was given the name from the latin "linum" (flax) and "oleum" (oil). Linoleum developed from the curious properties of linseed oil, which, when

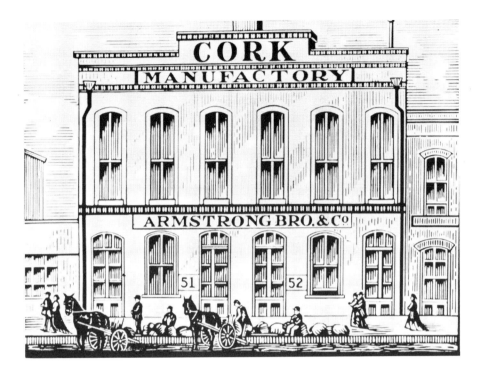

Pittsburgh plant of the Amstrong Cork Company prior to 1873.

exposed to air, dries out and becomes leathery. Unlike the earlier oil floor-cloths, built up by layer after layer of paint, linoleum was composed of dried, shredded and powdered linseed oil which was mixed with pulverized cork or sawdust, gums, and pigments, and then forced by enormous pressure into a burlap backing. This green linoleum was then hung in curing rooms and dried for one to six weeks.

Linoleum manufactured by Walton, and in the 1870s by Nairn, was imported into the United States. In 1869, Walton obtained patent number 87227, and began developing linoleum manufacture in New York, under the name of the American Linoleum Manufacturing Company, a subsidiary of the English concern. They were the sole exhibitors of American linoleum at the Centennial Exposition in Philadelphia in 1876. In 1886 they were competing with Nairn as well, who had set up a factory in Kearny, New Jersey for the manufacture of linoleum.

The United Roofing and Manufacturing Company in Marcus Hook, Pennsylvania, which manufactured "Congo" asphalt roofing materials, gradually developed a line of asphalt and felt-based, enamel-printed rug borders known as Congoleum. They were sold in 1911 as a competitive product for the inexpensive grades of linoleum. Their "Gold Seal" rug borders and floor coverings became a familiar trademark for many Americans. In 1924, the Congoleum Company merged with the Nairn Linoleum Company.

Two entrepreneurs, Thomas M. Armstrong and John D. Glass, in 1860 in Pittsburgh, Pennsylvania founded the Armstrong Cork Company, to manufacture bottle-stoppers. Quantities of cork chips and waste resulted from this manufacture. The chipped and pulverized cork residue left from this manufacture was found to be useable in other products such as gaskets and insulation materials. Cork is also an important raw material in linoleum, the manufacture of which the Armstrong Cork Company began at Lancaster, Pennsylvania, in 1909. In 1915, Armstrong provided its salesmen with pocket-sized pattern books, complete with definitions of the patterns and qualities available, and color plates of available stock. They offered heavy gauge battleship linoleum, backed with burlap, which complied with specifications set by the United States Bureau of Standards, in a variety of colors—gray, olive-green, dark blue, dark red and brown, as well as in inlaid square and diamond block patterns in off-white with dark blue, olive-green, blue-green and honey-gold, patterns in which the colors went through to the backing.

The Armstrong "Quaker" rug patterns. *Left to right :* floral, oriental, parquet. They are typical of the popular felt-base printed rugs widely used throughout the United States during the second quarter of the 20th century.

"Jaspe" patterned rugs with Chinese motif inspired by the rage for Chinese patterns during the late 1920s and reflecting a current fashion in woven carpeting.

Opposite :
"Home Sweet Home" painted by Charles Sheeler, 1931, showing carpets in a varied profusion of patterns. Such patterns were typical of 19th-century hooked rugs but have also been translated into 20th-century linoleum and Brussels carpeting.

"Jaspe" patterns, striated patterned linoleums, and "granite," a terazzo textured, were advertised during the 1920s and 1930s as a neutral base on which to throw rugs, of woven wool, hooked or braided, linoleum, or printed felt base.

In 1918, after launching their advertising campaign, "linoleum for every room in the house," the list of definitions was replaced with a listing of the rooms where linoleum might be used—bathrooms, bedrooms, dens, dining-rooms, hallways, kitchens and living-rooms.[23]

Printing and inlay processes improved and became more sophisticated. New colors and patterns were presented by all the manufacturers, in a wide variety of qualities, from the heavy, expensive battleship linoleums to the less expensive printed asphalt-saturated felts and papers. These printed rugs were often incorrectly known as linoleum rugs.

Linoleum was an outgrowth of the search for a more substantial type of

Opposite:
Panel of hand-woven two-ply ingrain carpet in the large repeated pattern so often depicted in paintings of that date. Believed to be English, *c.* 1830.

A process known as "inlaid linoleum" consisted of precise squares of shaped sections of linoleum composition cut out, fitted into the required pattern sequence on a burlap backing, and then subjected to enormous pressure thus bonding the surface and backing into a solid sheet of linoleum. During this process, the color went through to the backing.

Page 66:
The "Quaker Girl" trademark used by the Armstrong Cork Company on their printed felt-base "Quaker" rugs between the years 1927 and 1964 represented thrift, cleanliness and good housekeeping to the American public.

Overleaf:
High-style American bathroom *c.* 1950 with a fashionable "easy-care" linoleum floor in a pattern which was among the most popular of the Armstrong Cork Company's patterns from 1932 to 1974. It was known as pattern number 5352.

Various steps in modern
Rotograveur printing processes
for the decoration of resilient
floorings.

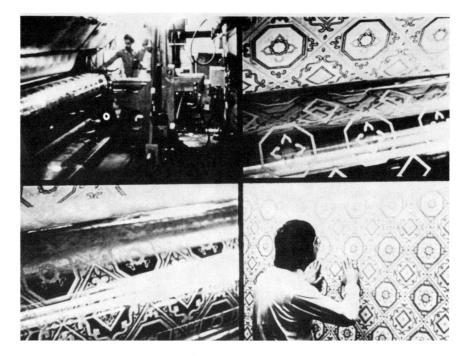

One of the enormous machines
used to print felt-base floor
coverings *c.* 1945. The pattern
imitates woven carpet patterns
fashionable at the time.

Two fashionable interiors, furnished with wicker and resilient floorings—separated by nearly half a century. The sitting room on the left, *c.* 1925, has a Congoleum rug, in an imitation oriental pattern; the one on the right, 1976, floored with wall-to-wall textured surface cushioned vinyl, reflects current taste in patterns.

floorcloth. And, within the linoleum industry, the terminology parallels that of the carpet industry. A linoleum "carpet" denotes a wall-to-wall covering of linoleum; a "rug" is an area-sized covering in standard sizes: 6 feet by 9 feet, 9 feet by 10½ feet, 9 feet by 12 feet. They were usually bordered, as were the prevailing styles in rugs, available from 1918 on, in a variety of patterns, which included oriental, geometric and parquet. An animal-pattern nursery rug was another example of this type.

Linoleum rugs were used throughout America from the 1920s on. Congoleum rugs, as did Armstrong's Quaker rugs, became household words. They were used in parlors and dining rooms of town houses, in farm communities, in mill villages. Often the floor surrounding these rugs was painted, leaving a raw board floor in the center of the room. These rugs were sometimes laid over a layer of newspaper on the floor, with the exposed boards painted yellow, ochre, dark red, or other colors. As one rug became worn, often a new one of the same size was laid directly on top, with a layer of newspapers between. A young woman from the Bronx recollected that in the 1950s the rugs were always in the middle of the floor, showing boards on all sides "so no one would think you swept the dirt under the rug. And it was cleaned with a weight—a heavy metal block with bristles on the bottom that had a handle—and you made it swing back and forth across the linoleum." She continued, "Everybody had them, especially the ones with big flowers and borders."

Care of linoleum was somewhat easier than that of floorcloths and carpets, and it was impervious to the ravages of moths and carpet beetles. Sweeping or mopping with an oil mop once a day was recommended, followed by frequent washing, one square yard at a time, using warm water and a mild soap, then polishing them every five or six weeks. However, linoleum had its disadvantages. The yellowing linseed-oil base prevented manufacture of a pure white

Trademark of a Congoleum rug.

color, and restricted the color palette. Continuing oxidation of the oils after years of use sometimes caused brittleness and cracking. Tannic acid in the cork, in combination with iron and humidity, caused rust rings if metal furniture stood on it. Heavy furniture made permanent indentations on the surface, and it did not react well with alkaline surfaces. But, for all these problems, linoleum had, by the 1920s, become a fashionable, easy-to-care-for, beautiful, sanitary floor covering. Patterns imitating bricks, terra cotta, leaf and floral motifs had depressed or embossed surfaces, accentuating the forms within the patterns. One, available in a red tile effect, and known by millions as Armstrong's "5352" pattern, remained one of the most popular kitchen-floor patterns in America from 1932 when it was introduced, until 1974, when the production of linoleum was suspended in favor of improved types of flooring.

As always, the quest for a more satisfactory substitute for an existing floor covering, combined with economic considerations and new technological developments, led to synthetic materials for floors. During World War II new plastics, vinyls, and other synthetics were developed and adapted to floor coverings. Known under numerous trade names as resilient floorings, these vinyl floor coverings, available in tiles or sheet, were now available in a whole new range of colors not possible in linoleums, because the vinyl base was colorless. Vibrant, pure colors, including white, became a new reality. Floors with a variety of textured surfaces which refract light and reduce the visibility of scuffs and scratches were now available. New "no wax" surfaces, when kept clean, maintain their high gloss far longer than other finishes. New waxes, providing cleaning and waxing in a single application, make these floors even easier to care for.

Many of these new resilient floor coverings have been developed with "do-it-yourself" in mind. Tiles, 9 or 12 inches square, of vinyl, asbestos, or asphalt, are easily put in place, some with adhesive already on the tile. Some of the resilient floorings can be simply laid on top of an existing floor or linoleum, no longer requiring skilled workers with special tools and adhesives to lay the rolls of heavy linoleum.

Another type takes advantage of an inherent quality of the vinyls, "plastic memory." Instead of using a backing in order to obtain a rigid material, a new product, developed by Armstrong, is an unbacked, cushioned vinyl flooring known as Tredway. It is pliable enough to be folded into a small package to be taken home, but quickly smoothes out when laid out on the floor. Held in place around the edges with staples, edges cut slightly too short can be stretched to fit. If a little too long, the edge is stapled in place anyway—and the material will contract to absorb modest excesses.

New technologies have made possible an enormous range of modern "floorcloths," underfoot in millions of American homes. They are a decorative floor in themselves, they challenge all the other floor coverings. They are not confined to a hallway or dining room—they can be found in any room in the house. Perhaps they are more frequently overlooked and stepped on than the oilcloths and floorcloths of the 18th and early 19th centuries, but they are part of the continuous fabric of social, economic and technological history of American floor coverings.

5 From Hand to Mechanized Loom: Carpet Construction

Although loom-woven goods were required for the production of floorcloths, and the simplest two-harness looms were necessary to weave list and rag rugs, the more elegant and fashionable carpet types—Ingrain, Axminster, Wiltons and Brussels, Chenille and Tufted, required advances in weaving and loom technology before they could be successfully, rapidly and economically produced. This chapter traces this transformation in a condensed form to provide some basic technological background, from the most basic flatwoven principles of hand weaving through the fascinating technology of the power looms—technology which is essential for an understanding of the construction of carpet fragments and examples. Understanding the construction also can provide clues to manufacturer, origins and identity.

Essentially, there are three basic construction techniques, each with its own history, subgroupings and refinements: Flatwoven carpets, Pile carpets, Tufted carpets.

Flatwoven

Flatwoven carpets, probably the oldest carpet form, were first produced on the simplest two-harness looms. Indeed there was no difference in construction technique between a linen sheet and a flatwoven carpet, except for the nature of the materials used.

"The Modern Wooden Hand-loom" c. 1840. Simple two-harness construction, suitable for making rag and Venetian carpets.

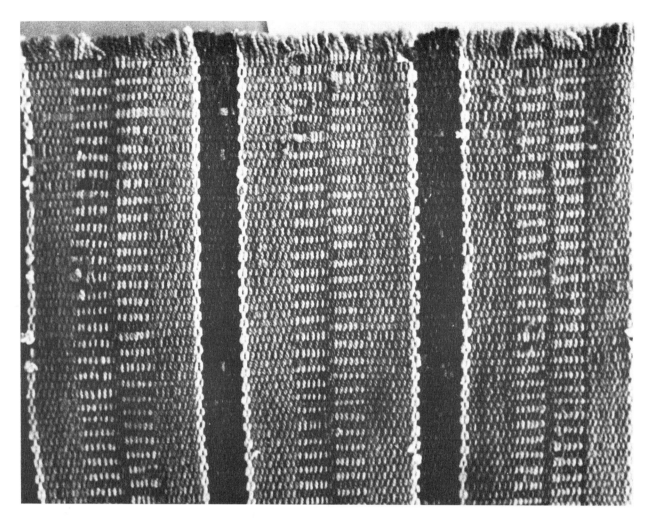

Detail of carpeting with closely spaced wool weft and rag filling.

In the two-harness loom, the warp threads, using strong cotton, linen or worsted yarns, are divided in two groups, A and B. Warp A is threaded through the heddles of the second one. When A is lifted, a space called a shed is formed from edge to edge through which the shuttle containing the weft is slid. Once the shuttle has passed through the shed, the weft is beaten against the already completed fabric with a reed, a comb-like device, and the warp is then reversed. This process is then repeated until the entire length of carpet has been obtained, or until the entire warp is used up. Simple patterns, stripes, checks, or solids are produced in this way.

Venetian and rag carpets are typical examples of the flatwoven carpet.

Venetian carpets, no longer produced commercially, are remembered for their radiant stripes in vivid colors. This effect was achieved by using brightly dyed warp threads, placed closely together, so close in fact, that they almost touched each other. Thus the warp provided the dominant color and permitted the continuous stripe along the whole length of the fabric characteristic of this carpet form. There is little evidence that such carpets were ever produced in Venice; like so many matters relating to carpets, the origin of the name is shrouded in mystery.

Rag rugs use a type of construction based on a scavenger concept—use of reclaimed and waste materials as the weft. In these carpets, produced as a sort of utility floor covering, the warp is set farther apart, to give the weft greater prominence. With a coarser weft, often dictated by the nature of the weft material, and a finer warp, the weft will provide the dominant color and texture.

Navajo carpets use the same two-harness loom technique common to all flatwoven carpets but, through a manipulation of the warp, the Indians managed to produce the stylized and geometric patterns of this native carpet creation of the Southwest.

Jerga carpets are a refinement of the plain flatwoven carpet brought about by introducing more harnesses and thereby dividing the warp into carefully calculated progressions. The end result of this technique is a fabric identical on both sides. Twill and herringbone design patterns are characteristic of this construction.

Ingrain carpets, the most ambitious of flatwoven carpets, present colors and patterns that reverse on the back. This is achieved by complicated and sophisticated modifications of the loom—numerous different harnesses on a draw loom are used to control the warp. One of the most immediately recognizable characteristics of this type of carpet is the air pockets in between the front and back in the large woven areas of the pattern. This happens when the warp is set up with two colors alternating, for example red and green, and labeled green 1, red 1, green 2 and red 2 in repeated sequence across the width of the loom. By raising green 1 and inserting a green weft, raising green 2,

red weft 1
warp 1
red weft 2

green weft 1
warp 2
green weft 2

Cross-section of two-ply ingrain carpeting. Where red weft 1, red weft 2, green weft 1, green weft 2 cross, the top and bottom layer are joined, and the color reverses.

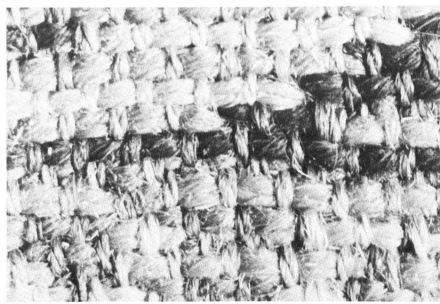

Detail of ingrain carpeting. The warp is fine, two-ply worsted; the weft is double strands of yarn treated as a single weft. In some ingrains a single, thick yarn is used for some colors in the weft, two thinner yarns for others.

Cross-section of three-ply ingrain, showing how the three separate layers are interlocked. The process was developed in Scotland in 1824, and permitted more complicated patterns than two-ply ingrain.

and again inserting a green weft, etc., a solid green fabric would be formed, but the red warps would not be integrated into the fabric, and would simply remain warps. If red had been chosen instead, and combined with a red weft, a red fabric would have been produced. It follows then that by first controlling the red warps and inserting the red weft, then inserting a green weft between the green warps and then red again, two separate but identical fabrics would be formed. If the warps were so arranged in the loom that the greens were raised along only one half of the loom, and the reds were raised on the other half, the colors would reverse in the center. By very careful calculation of the red and green harness patterns from top to bottom, geometric and floral patterns can be formed. Producing this type of carpet is not without problems. The areas with air pockets are more susceptible to wear, and therefore details of the patterns should interlock as frequently as possible. To achieve such interlocking the Jacquard attachment is used which applies two sets of identical pattern cards, one to control the upper side pattern, the other the lower side.

Pile

Axminster. Pile carpeting originated hundreds of years ago in Turkey and Persia, from where it was brought to Europe, to be promptly imitated.

Spun wool yarns in different colors are knotted to a warp to form an upright tuft, which is held in this upright position by one of several wefts. The resulting surface of the carpet can be compared to a wheatfield with all the fibers literally standing on end. The vertical direction of the cut or looped pile yarns distinguishes pile carpets from ingrains.

The specific knotting techniques of Turkish and Persian carpets were fully understood and imitated in Europe long before they were brought to America by the early settlers. The Turkish and Persian knots—which differ from one another—are shown on page 124. The English hand-knotted products known as Axminster carpets and based on the Middle Eastern forms were first produced during the 18th century.

The earliest American pile carpets were hand-knotted Axminsters still clearly copying the Middle-Eastern knotting techniques. But it was soon realized that the slow, time-consuming, hand-knotted construction was commercially self-defeating in a country that needed mass-produced goods at low prices. The first hand-knotted Axminsters were produced in the United States in around 1790, but the search began for a construction technique that would duplicate the appearance of the hand-knotted Axminster, yet could be produced by a mechanized loom. It was not until 1867 that a satisfactory

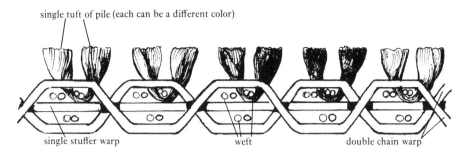

single tuft of pile (each can be a different color)

single stuffer warp   weft   double chain warp

Cross-section of Axminster which has three sets of double-shot weft, a single stuffer warp yarn, and a double-chain warp. In this weave, the pattern is partially visible from the back because the double-shot weft underneath alternates with the pile. This also creates a slightly ribbed surface on the back.

Spool Axminster loom, still in use in the United States. (The individual colored yarns can be seen on the spool.) In England a similar type, known as a Gripper Axminster loom, is used.

mechanized loom was produced by Halcyon Skinner in Yonkers, New York. He utilized some of the concepts of the mechanized power loom invented by Erastus B. Bigelow in 1839, but added to the Bigelow loom the endless chain.

The endless chain, a mechanism for the rapid production of pattern and color effects, was the technical advance that made it possible to speed up the basic power loom, so opening up the road to the mass-production of what became known as the Royal Axminster. Mounted on two powerful endless chain tracks, comparable to today's conveyor belts, were rolls or brackets, the width of the carpet, on which the pile yarns had been wound before the start of weaving. Each of them carried the colored pile yarns in the exact sequence for *one* row of pile, as dictated by the pattern. For example, for a 9-feet-wide Axminster with a 189 pitch there were 756 strands of colored pile yarn. Each of the brackets had attached to it a set of threading tubes, one tube for each of the strands of yarn in the pattern for that particular row of the carpet. The pile yarn ran through these tubes and protruded (like a fringe) from the threading tubes for a distance needed to produce the desired depth of the pile and a small additional predetermined overage. The length of the yarn was carefully

Preparation of the spools for
Axminster weaving. The table
behind the women contains
yarns on spools of all the colors
required for the entire pattern.
The spools are then placed on a
rod according to the pattern—
which can be seen on the roller
overhead—in order to make one
multi-colored spool, one for each
crosswise row of carpet.

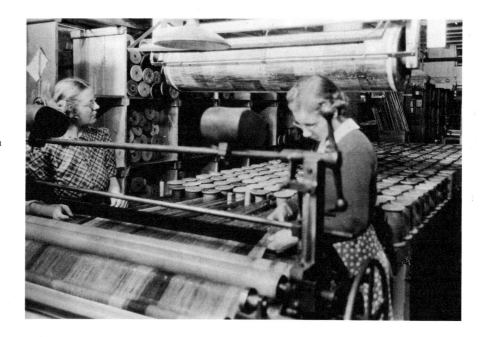

calculated to allow for the full length of the carpet. If in this example the pattern
would repeat after 36 inches, with seven rows of pile per inch, 252 brackets
were needed, and these were mounted on the endless chain.

The preparation of the yarns and spools for weaving was a tedious and time-
consuming task, requiring human labor, and to this day no satisfactory
substitute for this type of human labor has ever been found. This may be the
main reason why today Axminster rugs, requiring an inordinate amount of
hand work, represent less than 1 percent of the carpeting produced in America.

As with many carpet looms, cotton warp and stuffer yarns are threaded and
fed from the back of the loom by means of two or three beams. As one set of
warp is lifted to form a shed, the lowest bracket on the endless chain, directly
above the last finished row of woven carpet, is lifted from the endless chain
and moved forward and down by mechanized steel arms that guide the bracket
with its 756 threading tubes, from which the pile yarns protrude, and pushes
them through the warp very close to the last row of completed pile tufts.
Now the weft and filling shot, followed by the compressing action of the reed,
secures the protruding pieces of yarn thread. In the next progression, the
threading tubes and the bracket are now slightly lifted and move forward. The
end of the thread having been fastened to the carpet by this time is pulled
further through the threading tubes and doubles the pile above the weft. The
reed presses the row of weft and filler against the thread and ensures the secure
lodging of the pile with warp and stuffer.

As the bracket with the threading tubes is withdrawn, the spool unwinds
enough yarn to be ready for its next exposure to the warp, which in our example
would occur after the following 251 brackets had had their turn at the warp to
complete the pattern. Before the bracket returns to its predetermined place on
the endless chain, a scissor-like knife shears the yarn at the level of the pile
height that has been predetermined.

Nineteenth-century hand-operated Brussels loom which has a Jacquard for controlling the pattern. Behind the loom are five frames which contain spools of worsted warps for the pile.

Brussels and Wilton carpets were the luxury floor covering of the 18th and 19th centuries. The name Brussels is no longer used today, but the term Wilton has been preserved, and includes both styles, the looped Brussels and the Wilton. Today Wilton sales represent less than 0.6 percent of the total carpet sales in the United States.

Both of these carpets were made of dyed worsted fibers to produce an infinite variety of rich color and design combinations. The construction technique for both Brussels and Wilton, except for one minor detail, was identical, and was based upon the ingenious use of wires or metal strips, which determined the depth of the pile. The one difference was that Brussels had a loop surface, Wiltons, a cut one.

The looms on which these two types were woven were complex pieces of machinery, incorporating the Jacquard selector system, which manipulated threads running in the direction of the warp. The looms provided the standard linen or jute warp, a chain warp and stuffers. Between each warp thread, however, were inserted threads that contributed to the color and pattern. There were as many colored worsted yarns between each warp as there were colors required by one lengthwise row of the pattern. These colored threads were on spools and organized in flat boxes, called frames, one for each color. From the frames, which were positioned horizontally behind the loom, were drawn the threads in the colors demanded by the pattern. Each worsted yarn spool ideally contained enough thread for the whole length of the carpet without knotting, which always presented problems.

So as to avoid crowding the space between the warps, there were seldom more than six different colors employed. In those rare instances where the pattern demanded more than six colors, the additional colors were inserted by a special substitution process called "planting."

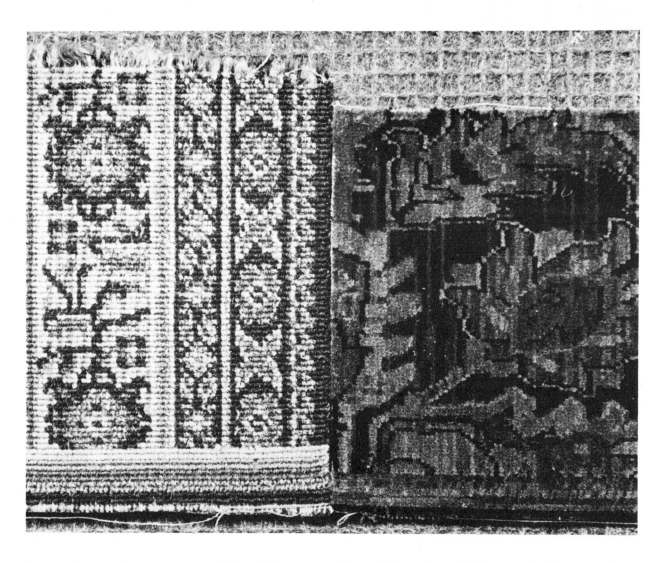

Early-20th-century Brussels (*left*) and Wilton (*right*). The striped lines along the bottom edge of the samples are guides to planting, that is, substitution of additional colors into the carpet without increasing the number of frames. The five-frame Brussels (five stripes) has a total of six colors, added in the third stripe which alternated red with a bluish green.

Each of the yarn spools would be activated for its part in the pattern by a thread selection device, the "heddle frames," usually operated by an assistant—often children working with the weaver.

To produce the pile effect in both the Brussels and the Wilton, wires or metal strips of varying width and thickness were temporarily woven into the carpet. These metal parts were slightly longer than the full width of the finished woven material. After each warp change two wefts were passed through the shed for Brussels and three for Wilton to give the carpet strength and body. The number of metal strips inserted per inch was a measure of the quality—six insertions per inch meant a coarse product, twelve was the mark of superior quality.

After about ten or twenty rows, each containing the metal strip, had been woven, the first metal strip was withdrawn from the back and placed into the front. This process is endlessly repeated as the weaving progresses, just as in a children's game of "stack the hands," where the bottom hand is forever withdrawn and replaced on the top.

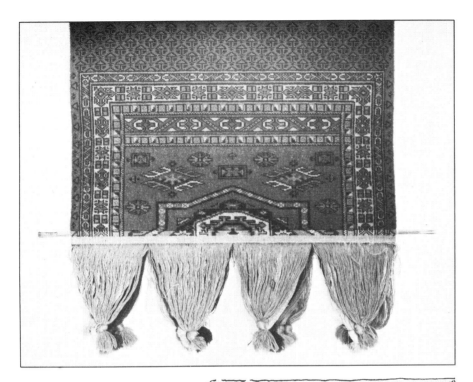

"Whittall Anglo Persian" Wilton in process. The upper portion is a 27-inch width of finished cut-pile carpet; the four wires originally inserted can still been seen. Each one has a knife blade on the right-hand end which will cut the loops when the wire is withdrawn. The four sets of warp yarn required in its manufacture hang below: colored yarns for the face; two sets of cotton warp yarn which, with the weft, forms the structural fabric; and a third cotton stuffer warp for added body.

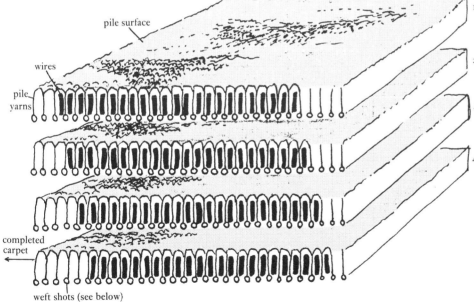

pile surface

wires

pile yarns

completed carpet

weft shots (see below)

1

2

3

4

Diagram of the progression of the removal and replacement of wires in Brussels and Wilton. Series 1–4 shows four consecutive rows of carpet. The last wire, when removed, becomes the first.

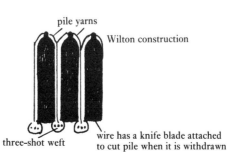

Brussels construction

pile yarn

looped pile

wires   two-shot weft

pile yarns

Wilton construction

three-shot weft

wire has a knife blade attached to cut pile when it is withdrawn

Two mid-19th century carpet
bags: the one on the left is made
from Brussels carpeting, the one
on the right from tapestry velvet.
Compare the differences in
precision of the patterns: this
depends on the relative
difficulty of controlling the
pattern on the printed warp.

Cross-section of the three-frame
Brussel carpet, which has two
shots per wire and one stuffer
yarn. Colors which do not
appear on the surface are
carried along within the carpet
structure.

In the Brussels, the withdrawal of the wire produced the loop, which is its
trademark. In the Wilton, the metal strip is slightly modified by having a sharp
knife attached at the top of one end, and as the metal strip is withdrawn, it
slits the loops and produces Wilton style pile.

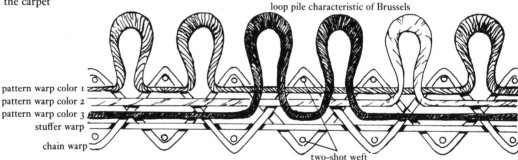

Cross-section of a three-frame,
three-shot Wilton, with one
stuffer yarn.

A further refinement of the Brussels carpet was the preprinting of the warp
on giant drums with calculated patterns, so that when woven over the wires,
the printed pattern appeared.

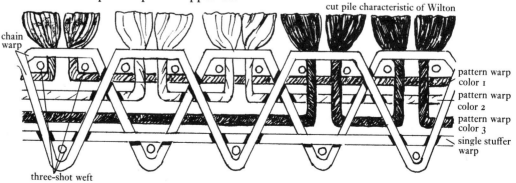

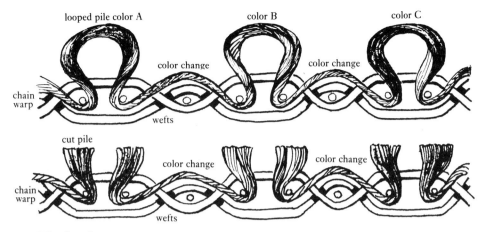

looped pile color A color B color C

color change color change

chain warp

wefts

cut pile

color change color change

chain warp

wefts

Cross-section of tapestry Brussels (*top*) and tapestry Wilton (*bottom*). Only a single pile yarn is required for each lengthwise row of the pattern, since the yarn is printed with various colors in carefully calculated progressions before weaving.

Tufted

Forerunners of the tufted carpet were both tufted bedspreads and bathmats. After World War II, the tufted carpet came into its own, and today about 90 percent of all carpets manufactured in the United States are tufted. The process is adaptable in terms of color use and design, and even through manipulation of the length of the loops to produce contour patterns.

Actually the tufting process is an adaptation of the sewing-machine stitch to carpet production. It can most readily be explained by showing the action of a single needle. The drawing below explains the loop formation for both short

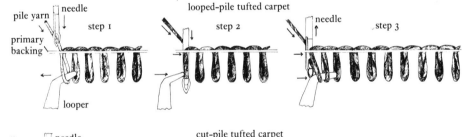

a

pile yarn needle looped-pile tufted carpet needle

primary backing step 1 step 2 step 3

looper

a. Progression of the needle, looper and yarn to form looped-pile, tufted carpets.

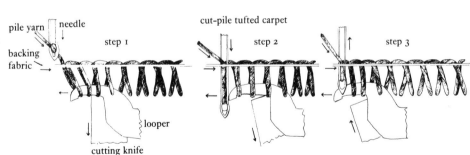

b

pile yarn needle cut-pile tufted carpet needle

backing fabric step 1 step 2 step 3

looper

cutting knife

b. Looper mechanism with a cutting blade for making cut-pile tufted carpets.

loop tufting and cut pile tufting.

The tufting loops are attached to a fabric backing, usually some woven material. The backing into which the tufting is stitched is pulled past the needles at a speed that permits between 5 and 10 stitches per inch depending upon the thickness of the yarn and the density of the finished product desired. The spacing of the needles varies from $\frac{3}{16}$ inch to $\frac{5}{64}$ inch between tufts. Accordingly, from 5.3 to 12.8 tufts per inch can be produced. For various patterns, different colored yarns can be fed to each of the stitching needles. Carpets of a uniform color are usually manufactured from undyed yarns and subsequently dyed in large vats.

The machines that produce these tufted carpets have a needle bar with from

Needle used in a tufting machine. This is but one of numerous needles of different sizes used for tufting carpets.

1016 to 2434 needles for a 15-foot-wide carpet. They can make as many as 500 consecutive stitches to complete per minute 2 yards of 15-feet-wide tufted carpet.

Once the carpet is produced and dyed, the back is coated with a latex solution, stretched and pasted to a separate backing. During drying in a heating chamber, the latex is cured and bonded to the separate backing material, which has now become an integral part of the finished product.

Various components of tufted carpet. The face yarn is stitched into the primary backing in the first process, then the secondary backing is applied with latex.

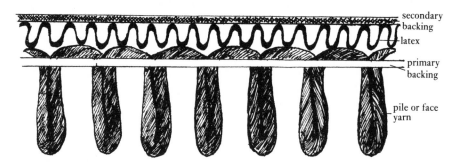

secondary backing
latex
primary backing
pile or face yarn

One of the needles used to mat the fibers together to produce the felted, needle-punch carpet.

The **needle-punch** carpet, a technological discovery of 1960, is neither a woven nor a needle-stitched carpet. It is a floor-covering which resembles felt; staple fibers are entangled in such a manner that the closeness of the fibers supports them in an upright position. The effect of a needle-punch carpet can be simulated by taking a paint brush and pressing the bristles together so as to produce an almost solid surface. To bring enough fibers next to each other, the needle punches as many as 800 to 1,200 times through a square inch of fabric, pulling fibers to each side of the scrim that holds them.

The needle-punch carpets are produced with needles that carry no thread, but have barbs that entangle the fibers as they come into contact with the needle.

The process may be described as follows. On several conveyors, fibers are arranged in a random fashion to form a blanket-like coverage. Several of these layers are superimposed upon one another to make a thick, loose bat. A woven piece of material (the scrim) is now inserted between the upper and lower bat of fibers. The bats are tacked and evened out before they are fed into the needle punch machine, which consists of two plates. The lower of these plates contains numerous holes which correspond to barbed needles that are fastened to the upper plate. As the batting and the woven material (scrim) that separates the two bats is moved over the lower plate, the upper plate with the barbed needles moves downward and pushes fibers, which the barbs engage, through the scrim. On the upward motion of the barbed needle, the fibers are engaged from below the scrim and brought upward. The process is repeated at great speed, with the material moving slowly over the lower plate, and thus permitting countless penetrations.

Opposite:
Separate "leopard" spotted border on ingrain carpeting gives a rare glimpse of the colors and pattern combinations considered fashionable in the early 19th century.

Once the fibers are placed by this technique into the scrim material, it is shorn to produce a uniform surface. The opposite side is coated with a foam rubber base, if the carpet is to be used for indoor use, or with a latex coating which is more suitable for outdoors.

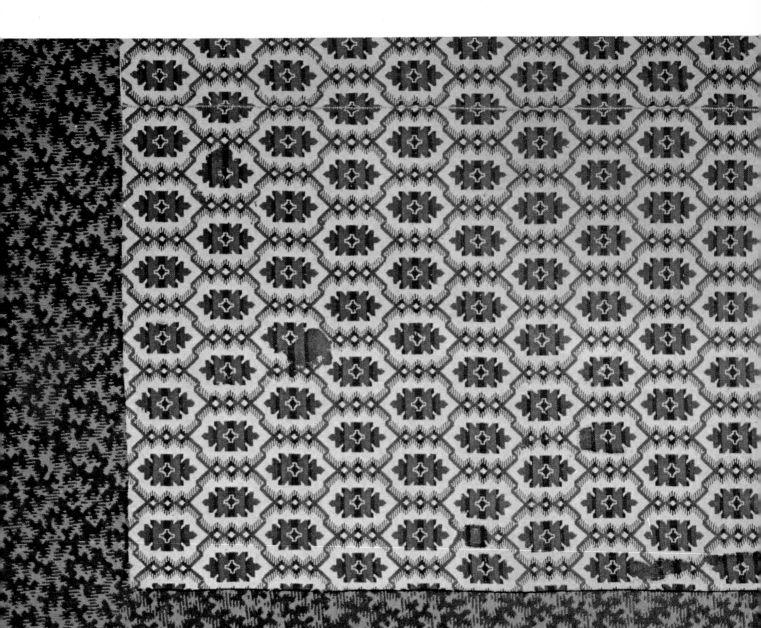

Although produced as a luxury carpet in Scotland from 1840 on, the process of **chenille** carpet manufacture was brought to the United States only in 1910, and found only a brief acceptance. Today chenille carpets are a curiosity of another age and are no longer made.

They can be produced in a wide variety of colors and designs. Their manufacture requires a two-loom process, the first for the production of the chenille blanket which, after cutting apart and folding, will provide the pile for the woven carpet. The second process produces the woven pile carpet. In the first process the chenille blanket is made, essentially of flatwoven fabric with wefts of worsted yarn held together by groups of six fine cotton warp threads which form spines. Each group is separated by $\frac{1}{2}$ to $\frac{3}{4}$ inch (see drawing). The worsted wefts in Process 1 are arranged in carefully calculated, alternating sequences based on the width of the finished carpet. For example, at every 16 feet there would be a red marker thread to indicate the end of a row. The pattern sequence for the first width is arranged from left to right, the second width from right to left and so on. The pile required for an entire carpet is woven on the first loom.

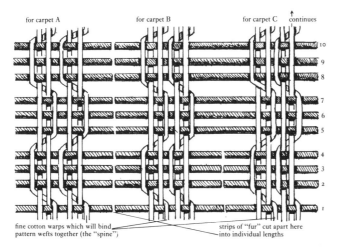

for carpet A   for carpet B   for carpet C   continues

fine cotton warps which will bind
pattern wefts together (the "spine")

strips of "fur" cut apart here
into individual lengths

Then this blanket is cut apart into strips on either side of the spines as indicated below. Each strip of fur will provide the pile for a separate identical carpet. These strips of fur are steamed and folded along the spine and then wound on to enormous shuttles in preparation for Process 2. In Process 2 the strip of chenille fur is hand-inserted as a pile of weft into the shed of the second loom on which the carpet is made. The marker threads at the ends of rows and all the tufts between are carefully adjusted by hand to form the pattern. Then a cotton catcher thread (warp) fastens the fur into the main body of the carpet as shown in the drawing. The carpet is built up by this process, row by row.

The technical development of American carpet-manufacture over the past 150 years embraces various forms and countless ingenious manufacturing devices. All these inventions were in reality sparked off by the never-ending quest for production economies and product improvements that would appeal to the consumer. And so, usually with the added stimulus of competition, the product became ever more widely available—a carpet for every American floor.

Page 86:
Responding to public demand, Navajo weavers began incorporating pictorial subject matter into their rugs in the 1880s. This rug, of handspun wool, was woven in New Mexico during the first half of the 20th century.

Overleaf:
"The Old Clock on the Stairs" painted by Edward Lamson Henry, 1868. Striped rag carpeting, patterned damask Venetian stair carpeting, a shaggy or fur mat at the foot of the stairs and a floral-patterned sitting-room in a well-appointed house of the period.

Process 1. The weft pile yarns are woven according to the pattern, then cut apart, folded and wound on enormous shuttles. In the second process, these wefts will provide the first ten tufts (from left to right) in a single crosswise row of pile. A single weft blanket will provide pile for numerous different looms.

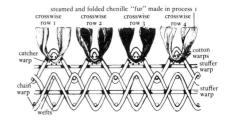

steamed and folded chenille "fur" made in process 1

Process 2. Shows the woven, steamed and folded "fur" inserted into the body of the carpet.

Opposite:
One of the Venetian striped carpets manufactured by E. C. Beetem and Son of Carlisle, Pennsylvania from 1876 to 1953.

6 Flatwoven Carpets

Ingrain

Scotch, Kidderminster, Kilmarnock, English ingrain, Venetian, spotted and mottled were all familiar carpet terms in America in the 18th and 19th centuries. They referred to reversible, patterned carpets with a flatwoven surface without a pile, made entirely of new materials. Differences in name resulted from various localities of origin, from varieties of flat weaves, and from methods of dyeing the wool.

Kidderminster was a 17th-century textile center southwest of Birmingham, England, where the earliest ingrains (see pages 73ff.), often referred to by that name, are believed to have been woven about 1735. Kilmarnock, a carpet center near Glasgow, Scotland, also gave its name to the carpets woven there. "English" and "Scotch," probably identical in pattern and construction, were simply identified by country of origin.

These carpets were being imported into American port cities—Boston, New York, Annapolis—by the mid-18th century. There is evidence of new "English Carpets" for sale in Annapolis in 1752.[1] In the same year some English bed carpets were stolen from a shop window in Boston. In 1760, "Kilmarnock Floor-Carpets from 5 to 21 square yards" were advertised.[2] They were also of sufficient value to be mentioned as "1 old Scots [Carpet]"[3] in the 1761 inventory of William Hunter, a printer from Williamsburg, Virginia. Such carpets were sold at public sales and auctions throughout the 18th century. When household goods of the Honorable John Penn were auctioned in Philadelphia in 1788, ". . . a Scotch carpet and 2 bed [side] ditto, new" were included.[4]

In the 18th century great strides were made in weaving when two English inventions made it possible to weave fabrics patterned, and wider than before. In 1733 John Kay, a Scottish weaver, invented the fly shuttle, a device which catapulted the shuttle across the warp faster and further than one could do it by hand. In 1760 he introduced multiple shuttle boxes, each of which could hold a shuttle of differently colored weft yarn, and which made multicolor weft patterns easier to control and weave, since the shuttles did not have to be changed each time new colors were needed. By the third quarter of the 18th century, these new processes meant that ingrain carpeting was available in quarter, three quarter, yard and six quarter or 54-inch widths, giving a considerable variety for stairs and hall widths.

At this time weavers were sought in Norfolk, Virginia to operate "one Loom Counterpanes 10 quarters broad."[5] Many skilled weavers, particularly Scottish,

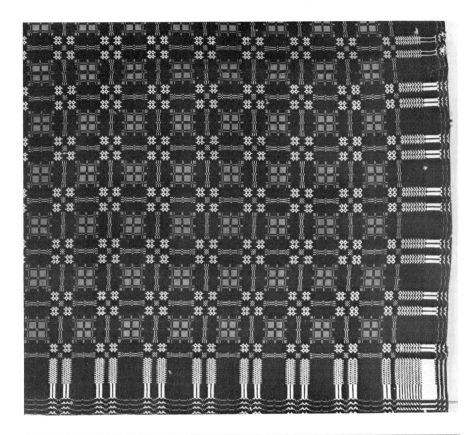

Red orange, navy and white coverlet which, if woven in slightly heavier yarns, may have been used as a floor covering. The pattern resembles the floor covering in the portrait of John Phillips.

"John Phillips" painted by Joseph Steward, 1777. This portrait shows that the sitter was one of the fortunate individuals who had several decorative floor coverings in his house.

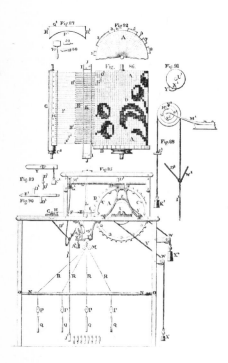

The Barrel loom, which used the principle of a music box to control patterns, was an early-19th-century alternative to the Jacquard.

Opposite:
Complicated floral and curvilinear carpet patterns in a large scale were prevalent during the second quarter of the 19th century after the invention of the Jacquard, which enabled them to be woven more easily. This late-19th-century Canadian Jacquard carpet could be easily mistaken for a coverlet in pattern and coloring.

came to America during the late 18th and early 19th centuries and settled in Philadelphia in an area known as Kensington in the Northern Liberties. One of the earliest recorded carpet weavers in Philadelphia was William Calverly, who had set up shop by 1775. It is not known, however, whether some of his carpets were ingrain. The small shop—with three or four, but never more than a dozen, weavers—operated on the European system which they had left behind in the Old World. Raw materials were received, dyed and woven at the shop, then picked up as finished carpets by the "manufacturer" responsible for the collection and sale of the carpets. This type of "store" continued throughout the 19th century.

It was difficult to weave carpeting evenly by hand, so that the pattern repeated at an exact length. For this reason, many early carpets are somewhat mismatched at the seams.

Occasional references were made to the patterns and colors of 18th- and early-19th-century ingrains. One, advertised in a 1790s newspaper advertisement, reads: "English ingrained, of superior quality, both black and green grounds."[6] It is possible that this carpeting may have been similar to that shown in the portrait of Mary Floyd Tallmadge, painted by Ralph Earl in 1790, with a dark-green background and pattern in red, black and white in the collection of the Litchfield Historical Society, Connecticut.

One floorcloth manufacturer from Pennsylvania, Isaac Macaulay, began to expand his business to include carpets. He brought skilled workmen from Kidderminster to work on his two-ply ingrain looms and by the 1820s was well enough established to weave ingrain carpeting for the Pennsylvania state capitol in Harrisburg.[7]

There were constant efforts to improve the looms, to enable faster, less expensive, more accurate production of carpeting. Before the invention of the barrel loom about 1815 which operated on the principle of a music box drum to control the warps, and the perfection of the Jacquard pattern-weaving mechanisms, ingrain carpeting with its interlocking, reversible patterns was woven on multiple-harness looms, some of which were controlled by a draw loom mechanism. The perfection of the Jacquard attachment in 1804 by the Frenchman, J. M. Jacquard, and its subsequent adaptation to carpet weaving was a major breakthrough in carpet technology (see also page 117).

It was introduced in Philadelphia, applied to ingrain weaving and remained a secret closely kept by the weavers, who were far better paid than those in other weaving centers. According to legend, Alexander Wright, the manager of the Medway, Massachusetts carpet mill, went to Philadelphia to learn about this new attachment. Unable to obtain the information there, he went to Scotland, where the Jacquard device had been in use. Here he acquired the Jacquard attachments and also managed to hire the weavers to operate them.[8]

In the two-ply ingrain construction, the colored patterns were exactly reversed. The invention of three-ply ingrain carpeting in England in 1824, with two Jacquard mechanisms needed to produce it, created more complex patterns in a luxurious, longer wearing carpet, with the reverse completely different from the front. These rugs were imported into the United States but, by 1833, were also produced domestically by the Thompsonville carpet

factory, in which a special section had been set up strictly for the production of three-ply ingrains.[9]

Although there had been manufacture of various kinds of carpets on a small scale in Philadelphia and in New England during the early 19th century, it was during the mid-1820s that the American carpet industry was born. A series of new tariff laws imposing duties on imported carpets were enacted, thereby encouraging the small, individually owned, domestic carpet manufacturer to expand. At the time there was an infant cottage industry, largely centered in Philadelphia, of which William Sprague was perhaps the most important member.

The new tariff protection provided a climate favoring American entrepreneurs who could now enter a market the size of which they could only sense. They realized how the rich longed to improve their homes with expensive imported carpeting.

Almost from the beginning the wealthy in America purchased carpets and, since so few were produced at home, they turned to imports. An early advertisement of A. and E. S. Higgins, an importer and dealer with a warehouse on Pearl Street in New York, shows the range of merchandise that was available:

Royal Wilton, Three Ply, Double Super, Superfine, fine Ingrain, Venetian Hall and Stair carpeting, Table and Piano covers, Turkey, Tufted, Brussels and Wilton hearth rugs, Druggetts, Baizes, Mattings, Round, Oval and flat Stair Rods, &c. &c. Also, an extensive assortment of English and American Floor Oil Cloth, from 2 to 24 feet wide.[10]

Now the protection of the new tariff laws had created an economic climate favorable to the development of a domestic carpet industry, one which throughout the 19th century was dominated by ingrain production. In the years that followed, Americans entered this infant industry to create and develop a market for the new luxury commodity: CARPETS.

Stephen Sanford, E. S. Higgins, Orrin Thompson, and Erastus Bigelow were the earliest of the new carpet manufacturers. They set up large-scale operations in New England, and were followed within the next decades by Alexander Smith, Charles Masland, James Magee and the Shuttleworth Brothers—names still found today in the Who's Who of the carpet industry. Most of these firms first produced ingrains, then diversified into the manufacture of other types.

Although Philadelphia had a small group of carpet weavers from the earliest beginnings, the companies that ultimately became the giants in the industry chose New England and New York state for their production sites.

The Lowell Manufacturing Co. of Lowell, Massachusetts in 1828 purchased a small three-year-old mill in Medway, Massachusetts, and enlarged it. Within four years it employed nearly 150 people and produced during the year an astonishing 110,000 yards of hand-woven carpets, both ingrain and Brussels.[11]

John Sanford, one of the major northern manufacturers located in Amsterdam, New York, started with the production of ingrain carpets. Gradually he,

Five samples of 19th-century hand-woven carpeting, typical of the more readily available types. *First two rows:* Venetian striped. *Center:* overshot coverlet weave. *Bottom:* plain woven plaid wool ("common carpeting"). *Right:* hit-and-miss rag.

like many others—probably under the impact of competition—diversified and went into Brussels, tapestry carpets and finally into Axminsters, for which he is most remembered. He was the first to use broad looms for the manufacture of Axminster "gotten up especially for the introduction of oriental effect."[12] "Beauvais," the trade name for Sanford's Axminster, had become so well established over more than fifty years as a brand name, that it was continued after Sanford and Bigelow-Hartford merged in 1929.

The rapidly enlarging manufacture of carpets in the early part of the last century required large factories and vast numbers of workers. The factories were built to house new massive looms and machinery, and with an abundant supply of highly trained weavers, most of them brought to the New World from English and Scottish centers, they soon began to mass-produce carpets in an ever-increasing variety of patterns, styles and designs.

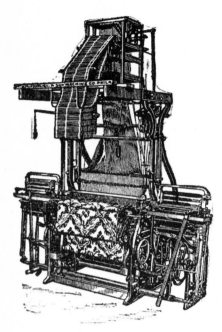

Power-driven two-ply ingrain loom with a single Jacquard attachment. A double Jacquard was required for weaving three ply, and additional Jacquards were necessary when weaving wide, one piece "art squares."

Opposite:
Extraordinary documented example of an imported English tapestry velvet carpet from "Acorn Hall" *c.* 1853. This elaborate medallion-motif carpet was woven on wide looms by John Crossley and Sons. It has a single center seam, and seams along the borders.

Alexander Smith, one of the early carpet pioneers, purchased a small mill in West Farms, New York, which had only 25 hand-ingrain looms in 1845. In 1850 he patented a type of two-ply "tapestry ingrain," in which both the warp and weft were pattern-dyed in a manner similar to the warp-printed Brussels carpets, producing a fabric which resembled the more elaborate three-plys. [13]

Realizing the limitations of the hand operations, he worked with Halcyon Skinner to improve their equipment. By 1856 they had invented a loom that "employed entirely new principles which though imitating handwoven Axminsters... produced in a manner greatly different than hand operations." [14] But it was not until 1867 that all the technical problems had been resolved, making the production of machine-woven Axminsters possible. When the Smith mill in West Farms burned down in 1860, the company moved to Yonkers, New York, where it continued until the 1960s. It was here that the first endless-chain mechanized loom in America, constructed by Halcyon Skinner, started operating in 1867.

By 1870 the rush of manufacturers into the carpet field had reached its peak. There were now about 215 firms producing a large variety of products. Competition became keen and many of the smaller companies could not keep up with the unending need for innovations, and product improvements and changes. By 1937 the number of American manufacturers in the carpet field was down to about fifty.

Since then there has been an upturn. There have been innovations in weaving techniques: the advent of the tufted carpet has created new fields of application never dreamed of before. Synthetic fibers have joined wool and cotton as the basic materials. Newcomers in the field like Coronet, Barwick, Cabin Crafts, Westpoint Pepperell and Milliken have made names for themselves, and joined the giants like Magee, Bigelow-Sanford Inc. and Lee, who are still active in a market that they started to develop well over a century ago.

Until 1840 all carpets manufactured in America were woven by hand, requiring the services of highly paid, skilled carpet-weavers. Because of the high labor cost, the end product was prohibitively expensive and finding a cheaper way to produce carpets soon became necessary.

The invention of the power carpet loom was encouraged by the need for more reliable, economic, faster methods of production. The man responsible for it was Erastus Bigelow, born in Boylestown, Massachusetts in 1814. When he turned to ingrain looms he had already invented a power-driven coach lace loom. Bigelow clearly understood what looms could do, and what could be accomplished by steam-driven machinery. He now set out to bring the two together. His first model, using steam, worked. But while this new power loom was indeed a radical departure from hand operation, it was not much faster than a hand-operated loom, on which a good weaver could weave eight yards of two-ply ingrain a day. But already in this early model several of the critical problems inherent in hand weaving had been overcome. Less skilled labor could be used; the length of pattern repeats was more consistent; the pattern was governed mechanically; there were even selvages, greater accuracy, and better matching. It was a beginning. Not until many improvements had been made, by the 1850s, could as many as 30 yards of carpeting be woven in a day.

Additional improvements followed quickly. In New England, large mills were filling the demand for ingrains on the power-driven looms, while in Philadelphia, most production continued on hand looms.

Even though Brussels and Wiltons were domestically produced as well as imported by the 1830s, ingrains were by far the most popular. Until the end of the 19th century, more than half the carpeting produced in the United States was ingrain. It was made in carpet and hall widths, and seamed to provide the fashionable wall-to-wall floor covering.

The 1870s saw some changes in carpetings. Large rugs which exposed the border of the floor, and one-piece ingrain carpets, became fashionable. Kendrick wrote in 1889:

> Within the past ten years surprising results have been obtained in ingrain weaving and designing. Prior to that, ingrain was classed among the lower grades of carpet, probably because its novelty had worn off, and it had reached the full perfection. English manufacturers, however, began to disprove this by sending over some remarkably beautiful specimens of ingrain art; squares, made of the ordinary ingrain yarns, but embodying such striking concepts in weaving, color and design, as to take them out of the realm of ordinary ingrain. Not only have these art-squares been cleverly reproduced here in Philadelphia, but the yard wide "extra super" carpet . . . has been greatly lifted in point of color effects and general appearance.[15]

Many years later, in 1902, Sears offered "new style" bordered rugs, "made with regular granite centers with handsome wide granite borders, with colored floral decorations to harmonize perfectly with the center, and each end of the rug is fringed"[16] for only $3.59. Ingrain, in a variety of patterns, was produced in American mills until the 1930s when it could no longer compete with the luxurious pile carpets. However, there has been a limited revival of ingrain production in the 1970s as reproduction carpeting for use in historic house renovations, and museum exhibitions.

Owing to the lack of genuine 19th-century carpeting today, the only way this style can be recreated in a contemporary house is by means of reproduction carpeting. Very few examples of historic carpeting exist and few existing ones are dated. There are various reasons for this. Carpeting wore out. Patterns continued unchanged for many years. Quantities of ingrain were lost during the Civil War; they were burned, cut up, or used as blankets for soldiers since ingrain was basically the same as many hand-woven coverlets. There is a record of one, which in the 1860s was taken from one of the literary society halls of North Carolina College, founded in 1853, cut into blankets, and sent to the soldiers of the Confederacy.

Another reason for the lack of early examples of ingrain carpets was the late-19th-century custom of cutting carpets into straight-grain or bias strips, and re-using them for the weft in a new rug. This type of rug, known as a fluff rug, ingrain carpet rug or Olson rug, must not be confused with the fluff mats or scrappy rugs, made from short strips in a knitted background. They were woven in Cincinnati, Philadelphia, Chicago and made at home, in widths from 18 inches to 10 or 12 feet.

Opposite:
"The Dinner Party" painted by Henry Sargent in the first quarter of the 19th century. A plain floorcloth, possibly baize or serge, was used to protect the center of the carpet under the table. In 1809 Thomas Jefferson had a green painted floorcloth serving a similar purpose in the south dining-room of the White House.

Ingrain carpeting from North
Carolina College, *c.* 1855 used as
a blanket during the Civil War.
On an accompanying note: "So
far as I know, this is the only
one now in existence. My father
Paul A. Barrie(s) used this one."

"Lee's Surrender to Grant" took
place in the parlor of the
McLean House in Appomattox,
Virginia, 9 April 1865. Although
the painting was not in existence
until the 1880s, the artist,
L. M. D. Guillaume, had been
to the house several times during
the intervening years to record
the interior. The distinct light
and dark stripe, in alternating
red and green, is a characteristic
of most ingrain carpeting of the
mid-19th century.

Detail of the "tweedy appearance with a velvet surface" of a fluff rug, woven from strips of old ingrain carpeting. Many fluff rugs had borders of ingrain which were of a different color from the rest of the rug.

Candace Wheeler, an artist-craftsman, described these rugs in 1900 as "undoubtedly the most useful—and from a utilitarian point of view the most perfect,"[17] in her book *How to Make Rugs*. She continued, "This type of 'rag rug' is made from worn ingrain carpet, especially if it is of the honest, all-wool kind, and not the modern mixture of cotton and wool."[18] After undoing the seams, the dirty widths were to be put in "a 'pounding barrel' and invited to part with every particle of dust which they have accumulated from the foot of man."[19] A pounding barrel was a large wooden barrel in which a plunger made of a stick with a block of wood attached to the bottom agitated the fabric. Another home procedure for cleaning these strips before reweaving was to put them outside on the lawn for several days at the mercy of wind and rain. They were then cut into strips about 1 inch wide, and sometimes raveled to make a narrow fringed or fluffy edge. The strips were used just as rags were, but a heavier warp of linen or hemp twine was needed.[20]

The overall effect of these carpets gives a tweedy appearance with a velvety surface, with bands of a slightly different color at either end. About three pounds of ingrain was required to make a square yard of carpet, and if desired,

the yarns removed from the raveling process could be wound into balls and used for another rug, or in the borders of the ingrain rug. "They lie where they are placed, with no turned-up ends, and this is a great virtue in rugs."[21] Through the last years of the 19th century and the early part of the 20th, manufacturers advertised a price rebate on any new carpet if the purchaser sent his old carpet with the new order. The system was good economics—the customer got rid of an unsightly old carpet, and the manufacturer had an inexpensive source of quality reprocessed materials. The Olson rug company offered this rebate until the mid-20th century.

Venetian

"Venetian" is a term used to describe a striped (but also sometimes checked) flatwoven carpeting which was a standard on the American scene from the late 18th century to the first decade of the 20th. (For construction details see page 74.) Webster's *An Encyclopedia of Domestic Economy* claims that "it is not known that what we call Venetian carpeting was ever made in Venice." It was usually striped although manipulation of the harnesses could produce checked patterns. It was, as Cole described it, "a low-grade floor covering of simple structure . . . The fabric is ornamented with stripes of various colors and widths, and is used as a cheap covering for halls, stairways and bedrooms. For many years the production of Venetian was an extensive and profitable branch of Philadelphia manufacture, but of recent years it has been largely supplanted by the lower grades of ingrain carpet."[22]

Venetian was possibly one of the earliest carpeting fabrics woven in America. It was advertised in New York in 1799 as a type of carpeting for sale at Norwood's carpet store in $\frac{1}{2}$, $\frac{3}{4}$ and $\frac{7}{8}$ yard widths, but it may at that time have been imported.[23] Striped carpets were woven in Massachusetts in the early 1830s; it is not certain whether they were list or Venetian. By 1834 damask Venetian was manufactured in Philadelphia where, along with ingrain, it was a major product until the 1880s, when it was replaced by the inexpensive ingrain carpeting.[24]

Although similar in structure to list carpeting, which used fabric strips for the weft, 19th-century Venetian carpeting used new materials, a coarse woolen or cotton warp, and a weft of jute or hemp. This two-ply fabric originally had, according to Cole, a woolen weft. In the carpet trade of the mid-1870s, Patent Imperial Venetian was available in all the usual widths for body and stair with either a wool or flax weft, and separate borders which were available for an additional price. By 1900 Venetian carpeting was still made but entirely of cotton.

Blankets and coverlets

In the 1890s, the Copp family of Stonington, Connecticut donated the collection of family textiles dating from 1750 to 1850 to the Smithsonian Institution. Among the items was a large, pieced, flatwoven reversible plain carpet in a muted orange and green, believed to have been woven by a professional weaver. This rug, and similar late-18th or early-19th-century examples in the collection of the Royal Ontario Museum, are of a type known as common car-

Opposite, top:
This two-ply ingrain carpeting with a damask or damask Venetian border from the Smithsonian Institution collection is very similar to the stair carpeting in the Currier and Ives lithograph. This particular example was patented by John Dorman Carpets in 1873.

Opposite, bottom:
"The Four Seasons of Life: Middle Age" by Currier and Ives 1868. The stair carpet, held in place with rods, could well be an ingrain carpet with a damask border, similar to that patented by Dorman in 1873. A deep pile mat of fur, or a shaggy rug, protects the floor covering where it meets the foot of the stairs. This is probably a painted floor oilcloth with a border which would have been harder wearing than ingrain carpet. Ingrains did not usually have borders in the 1860s.

Detail of the early-19th-century flatwoven carpeting, in yellow-red and olive-green check pattern, owned by the Copp family of Stonington, Connecticut. Strips of narrow fabric were stitched together to make a room-sized rug.

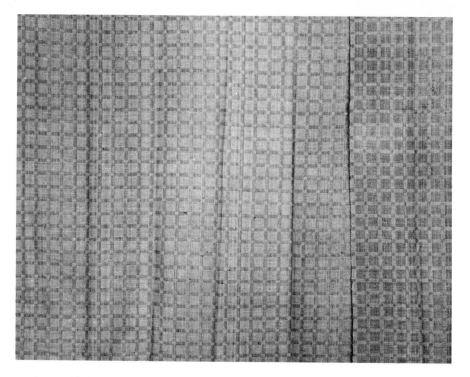

peting, which could be woven on a simple or common loom. Visually, and in construction, this type of carpet closely resembles two-color blankets of the period. Others were woven in overshot patterns which also appeared in the coverlets prevalent at the time. Documented examples of overshot carpeting in the Royal Ontario Museum found in the provinces of Ontario, Nova Scotia and New Brunswick show that carpeting of this overshot construction was also made and used.

It has been recorded that in the 19th century some bedrooms in parts of Nova Scotia, settled by the English, were furnished with matching overshot pattern carpeting and bed cover, although the colors of the items may have been different. There is, however, no evidence at this time that this was also a custom followed in the United States. Another piece in the Royal Ontario collection, woven in a small geometric overshot pattern with a faded-red warp and golden-brown and chartreuse weft, shows yet another pattern/color combination.

Weaving patterns, or drafts for carpeting exist. One is described by the Burnhams in their book *Keep Me Warm One Night* and the draft is labeled "English carpeting." Perhaps it is this type of carpeting which was referred to in the early shipping records and advertisements such as the one that appeared in the *Maryland Gazette* of 25 June 1752 for Turkey and English Carpets. In New York, Annapolis and other seaports during the 18th century numerous pieces of Scots or English carpeting were advertised for sale. References differentiate English and Scots carpets. Perhaps this distinction merely differentiated country of origin. Perhaps the distinction differentiated ingrain from overshot or other common loom constructions. Perhaps the weaving pattern for "English carpets" is a clue to pattern and construction differences based on country of origin.

Carpet fragment *c.* 1850 in overshot pattern.

In 1841, Rebecca Jaques' portrait was painted by Jacob Maentel. The floor of her room was covered with a checked floor covering. This could have been flatwoven "common carpeting" such as the Copps had; it would have been nailed to the floor at the edges.

If indeed English carpets were different from the other types of flatwoven carpeting, which the pattern draft name suggests, they would have had a different surface construction from the two-ply ingrain carpets. Ingrains are characterized by the woven pockets formed by the lack of interlocked areas in the carpet (see pages 74–5), an overshot on the other hand is characterized by fairly long floats of weft or warp which create blocks of color. The patterns likewise reverse on the other side, so that there is the opposite color in the pattern.

Nineteenth-century American coverlet weavers frequently advertised that they made carpets as well, and these reversible overshot patterns may quite possibly have been a common type. Overshot carpets were so similar to woven bed coverings that the possibility exists that some carpets which were not too badly worn were later used on beds.

Jerga

The Southwestern United States, primarily New Mexico, is the birth place of another flatwoven carpet, the "jerga." These carpets were used on the packed-dirt or oxblood-tempered floors, the most common flooring in the Southwest. (For construction details see page 75.) The word "jerga" originated in Arabia, where it appeared in a late-16th-century dictionary of Spanish and English, and was defined to mean "searge or sack cloth."[25] It was a thick, rough fabric. Jerga may well have been the fabric used on the floor, when a wealthy young suitor living in Mexico City listed a carpet of $7\frac{1}{3}$ varas in length, in various colors, among his possessions. Exchange with Mexico City was frequent, and just as people in the East cherished the imported possessions and adapted materials as substitutes, New Mexicans may have adapted the jerga for their floors as well, if imported carpets were too expensive. Usually twill-woven, but sometimes herringbone, on horizontal looms, jergas were made in widths ranging from 22 to 26 cm. and indefinite lengths. They were stitched together to make room-sized floor coverings. Locally grown wool was hand-spun into yarns about as thick as those used by the Navajos for weaving blankets, and either used in natural colors of creamy white, brown and black, or dyed with logwood or cochineal, a dye obtained from insects living on cacti, to produce red, or with indigo for blue. These colors antedate those made with aniline dyes, produced probably before the mid-1860s. Most examples of jergas, in patterns of stripes, plaids or checks, were woven with natural colors. In the neighborhood of Taos, New Mexico, according to oral history, jergas were always laid wall to wall, and tacked along the edges, over a padding of corn husks or over a layer of wool just as it was sheared off the sheep. A bit lumpy at first—but frequent footsteps would flatten it, and the underlay would give some protection against boots and shoes grinding the dirt into the carpet, and the carpet into the floor. Even so, such floor coverings were never as substantial as the worsted woven floor coverings prevalent in the East.

During the 18th century jergas, sometimes called gergas, were often found as floor covering in churches. Jerga was also used as a wrapping for goods sent from Sante Fe and Taos by pack train. In 1825–6, George Champlin Sibley, a surveyor from Missouri, listed "120 yds. Woolen Jerga at .20—$24.00"[26]

Hand-spun, twill-woven woolen fabric used as a floor covering, known in the Southwest as "Jerga." This late-19th-century example was woven in New Mexico.

along with canvas and rope. Interiors were also described by resident soldiers in letters and journals. In 1846 Captain Phillip St. George Cooke visited governor Manuel Armijo at the Palace in Santa Fe, New Mexico, describing the meeting room he entered from the hall as "a large and lofty apartment with a carpeted earth floor, and discovered the governor seated at a table, with six or eight military officials standing."[27] He also described the bedroom as "a long room looking upon the court, . . . the floor was carpeted, had one rude window, but a dozen at least of mirrors—a prevailing New Mexican taste."[28]

One of the best descriptions was written in an 1846 letter by Susan Magoffin describing the sala, or main room, of a house in Santa Fe in which she and her husband were living. "The floor too at the same end of the room is covered with a kind of Mexican carpeting; made of wool and colored black and white only. In short we may consider this great hall as two rooms for one half of it is carpeted and furnished for the parlor, while the other half has a naked floor, the dining table and all things attached to it at establishment to occupy it."[29]

Examples of jergas are in the collections of the Museum of International Folk Art in Santa Fe, and the Millicent Rogers Museum in Taos.

Nowadays, the term jerga is used in the Southwest, but its meaning has expanded from describing narrow-width hand-woven woolen floor coverings to include linoleums, rag carpeting, and factory-made carpeting. Rag carpeting was introduced into the area, but has achieved only limited success commercially.

Navajo

Of all American rugs and floor coverings, those of the American Indians, especially the Navajo, are the only genuinely indigenous ones. The origins of the weaving skills, and the designs, are typically suffused in myth.

According to Navajo legend, Spider Woman instructed the Navajo women how to weave on a loom which Spider Man told them how to make. The cross-poles were made of sky and earth cords, the warp sticks of sunrays, the healds of rock crystal and sheet lightning. The batten was a sun halo; white shell made the comb. There were four spindles: one a stick of zigzag lightning, with a whorl of cannel coal; one a stick of flash lightning with a whorl of turquoise; a third had a stick of sheet lightning with a whorl of abalone, a rain streamer formed the stick of the fourth, and its whorl was white shell.[30]

The Navajos had not always been weavers. The craft of weaving requires a permanent existence for cultivation of fiber, harvest, and spinning. Originally the Navajo were nomadic. They were latecomers to the Southwest, arriving during the 16th century and settling in south-central Colorado and northern New Mexico. Their neighbors were the Pueblo Indians, living in multi-level adobe dwellings, raising corn and especially cotton, which they had grown perhaps since A.D. 700 to produce exceptionally fine textiles. Sheep, along with horses and cattle brought to the New World by the Spanish conquistadores, were introduced to New Mexico by Don Juan de Oñate, the Governor and Captain General of New Mexico in 1698. Now wool could be used in the weavings as well. Pueblo men were skilled weavers, working on upright looms in their houses or out of doors. The Navajo women acquired their skill from them. They used only wool, and the earliest weaving was devoted to making wearing apparel—blankets or primitive striped patterns that reflected an earlier Pueblo style.

The Navajos, as nomads, had horses, acquired through trade, war or theft, and rapidly increased their herds of sheep by similar tactics. Living in small semi-nomadic clans, in circular or hexagonal wood or stone structures with a conical roof and the door facing east, they sought better pastures for their sheep.

Navajo women, having learned the techniques and first patterns from the Pueblo Indians, soon developed a distinctive style of their own. Their skill was remarked on by Pedro Pino, a delegate to the Spanish Parliament who, in 1812, wrote in his *Exposicion de Nuevo Mexico*, "Their woolen fabrics are the most valuable in our province and Sonora . . . and Chihuahua as well."[31]

Fragments of their weaving, dating from the late 18th century, found in Massacre Cave in Canyon Del Morte, New Mexico, are the earliest existing examples of natural-colored handspun wools in stripe patterns.[32] Throughout the 19th century there were stylistic changes, incorporating diamonds, chevrons and their numerous variations, and color changes with the introduction of red yarns, dyed with cochineal or raveled from the red bayetta (baize) trade cloth.

Other changes took place as well. Navajo attacks on neighboring Spanish and Pueblo villages and thefts of sheep brought Captain Kit Carson and his soldiers to subdue them in 1863. Numerous circumstances combined to force the Navajo surrender. As a result many were imprisoned at Bosque Redondo, Fort Sumner, New Mexico, where they became acquainted with the cotton and Pendleton wool blankets so much easier to obtain than their hand-woven

Navajo weavers spinning yarn, and weaving on an upright loom. They wove without printed patterns or directions.

ones. Ultimately they returned to their lands, to raise corn and sheep and to resume weaving. But by then machine-spun wools and commercial dyes were available and the whole process was much faster.

There was demand for the blankets from the Mormons, who had set up trading posts at Lees Ferry on the Colorado River. Cowboys were avid purchasers of these blankets, often exchanging horses for them, and demanding larger sizes because they were better to sleep in. The 1880s brought the railroad to the Southwest. With it came machine-spun aniline-dyed Germantown wools in harsh greens, purples and other previously unknown shades; packaged dyes and cotton twine soon to be used for the warp in the blankets; and tourists. Trading posts sprang up along the railroad, offering more white man's goods in return for blankets.

The all-purpose Navajo weaving—once used for protective clothing, bed covering, door covering, floor covering—became a valuable tourist commodity.

C. N. Cotton, a former trader, established a wholesale Indian goods market in Gallup, New Mexico. With a mimeograph machine he printed advertising flyers and sent them to potential eastern buyers, hoping to stimulate interest for his wares. He wanted to reach the home-furnishing market, where rugs were becoming more fashionable than carpets, and his blankets could fit into the rug category.

Lorenzo Hubbell, trader at the Ganado trading post, was sufficiently interested in old patterns to hire E. A. Burbank, a painter, to make colored illustrations of them for use as patterns. Popular, saleable ones were shown to the Navajo weavers to provide inspiration. Borders, first seen on a blanket about 1873, and isolated pattern motifs reflecting the eastern craze for things "oriental," were encouraged. Hubbell was also one of the first to deal in special made-to-order room-sized rugs.

By the 1890s the Navajos, themselves wearing cotton or "Indian style" Pendleton blankets, wove mostly for trade. A profusion of gaudy colors, a cotton warp and loosely spun weft woven into bold patterns, were characteristic of their products. George H. P. Pepper, a member of the Hyde Exploring Expedition in 1896, had the following comments about the current weaving practices of the Navajo:

> What a commentary on our vaunted civilization. Primitive weaving in progress while analine dyes in a nearby receptical contaminate more wool. Hideous colours concealing a sister disgrace in the form of cotton warp. Fat envelopes within reach that need but the tearing of an end and lo the white man's dye is ready. And such dyes! Like a plague they have swept across Navajo land, breeding contagion wherever they went, and like the leprous discolorations they have marred the face of one of nature's children.[33]

At the turn of the 20th century, with railroad travel steadily increasing, the Fred Harvey Company obtained the railroad concession to provide travelers' amenities—food and newspapers. Favoring Navajo crafts, and exhibiting their rugs in stores throughout the country, he was particularly interested in establishing quality and fair prices for the blankets, purchasing only the best from the traders. He discouraged the use of cotton warp and Germantown yarns, and encouraged instead a return to the traditional methods of hand spinning, dyeing and weaving.

Today about 5,000 Navajo women still weave rugs. The craftsmanship and design are excellent, but sadly the craft is beginning to disappear. (For construction details see page 75.) Hubbell's trading post at Ganado has become a National Historic site. Both here, and in other reputable trading posts in the Southwest as well as in museum shops and fine stores throughout the United States, rugs of the old designs, characteristic of the various Navajo weaving districts, can still be found. Smaller and less costly is the banded rug, without borders, in the soft colors characteristic of the Crystal district near Fort Defiance, Arizona. The Storm Pattern, with flashes of lightning and storm symbols in strong colors—red, black and white, radiating from central geometric forms—represent the Tuba City area. The Yei and Yeibichai, with their tall, thin ceremonial figures, are from the Shiprock/Red Rock area, and are usually a fine tapestry weave.[34]

While most of the contemporary rugs employ some commercially dyed or dyed and spun yarn, the Two Gray Hills weaving depends entirely on soft natural colors and yarns, grays, blacks, and tans in dignified geometric patterns. Wide Ruins rugs use only vegetable dyes and are usually of particularly fine weaving.

The rugs of other less renowned districts, known in the trade as "general rugs,"[35] have no particular distinguishing characteristic. They may use hand-spun wools, are usually of a coarser weave and, though attractive, are less costly. The exceptions are the pictorial rugs, those that today include pictures not only of cows and horses, but of helicopters, American flags, pick-up trucks and railroad trains in their designs. These somehow particularly reflect the lively imagination which long ago led the Navajos, once they had acquired the skill of weaving, to experiment with design, devise elaborate patterns and adapt riotous colors and machine-made materials as they became available to an ancient craft.

Bordered Navajo rug, the only covering for a clay tile floor, was used by the architect Albert Kahn in 1918 as part of a fashionable interior for *Good Furniture Magazine*.

7 Brussels, Wilton and Tapestry

Brussels and Wilton carpets earned their place in the history of American floor covering by providing an ideal: they were luxurious, hard-wearing, hand-woven, expensive and beautiful—aspired to by many, but owned by the wealthy few. They were originally woven in England and were one of the first loom-woven carpets to be widely used in England and America. Because of close parallels in construction, patterns and historic development, they can be considered as a single carpet type. (For construction details, see pages 79ff.)

Brussels carpet, believed to have been invented about 1710 in Brussels, Belgium, is of looped-pile, woven construction. In the late 1740s a Brussels carpet factory was established in Kidderminster, England, by John Broome, who had learned from Belgian weavers the process of inserting round wires into the shed to produce a pile.[1] Within a few years, a Brussels variation with a cut pile, velvety surface was manufactured in Wilton, the name by which this carpet is still known. The patterned Brussels and Wilton carpets, woven on complicated hand-operated draw looms, were traditionally woven 27 inches wide, the width of the Flemish textile measure, the "ell."

Very limited yardage of Brussels and Wilton carpeting was produced by domestic looms during the 18th century in America. Production gradually increased during the early 19th century and they were manufactured at Macaulay's mill in Philadelphia in the early 1820s and by the Lowell Manufacturing Company in 1829, as well as by several other weavers.[2] Domestic production remained limited and costly until the invention of the power-driven Brussels loom in the late 1840s and its gradual acceptance and use.

Few examples of 18th- and early-19th-century Brussels carpet remain, and fewer still are documented. However, C. E. C. Tattersall, in *A History of British Carpets,* describes some of the patterns and colors of early Brussels carpets used in English houses: a deep red carpet with a motif of Royal Arms, believed to have been made for Carlton House in England still exists; on the floor in the Royal Pavilion at Brighton was a "geometrical diaper of flattened hexagon set both horizontally and vertically"; a third one was described as a "rich crimson and drab Persian pattern." Another pattern in the Pavilion galleries was composed of a "straggling floral pattern in green, red and yellow on a cream ground."[3]

Since transatlantic trade was brisk at this time, with many fashionable carpetings and furnishings being imported into America from England, it is

Opposite:
Bill to John Cadwalader of Philadelphia dated 1771 which included among other household furnishings costs for Wilton carpeting, thread and binding.

Brought forward — — — — — — £98..18..4

1771
January 5 To putting up a high post Chince bed & fixing 2 Ven: Cord: 0..7..6
Cloak pins & hooks 6/ — 12 Chince tassells @ 2/3 – 27/ — 1..12..0
To a Large Silk Ball: Tassell & line for the Lanthorn — 1..7..6
15th To a Large Sopha Stuff'd & finish'd in Canvis with the Materials
& a case made for D° — — — — — — 5..15..0

To 1 smaller D° — 16 hair 1/10 – 11½ Canvis 1/6 tacks 3/6
10 y.ds girth 3/4 — finishing d° in Canvis & making Case } 4..3..5
To an other D° — — — — — — — — 4..3..5
30 y.ds lace for binding 3 Sopha Cases — — — @ 4d — 0..10..0
An Easy Chair — finishing in canvis & making case 1..5..0
9 hair 16/6 — 9 y.ds Canvis 13/6 girth & tacks 6/ — } 2..3..5
thread & 10 y.ds silk lace — — — —
To making 6 chair cases tied & white fringed thread & tape } 0..12..0
15 y.ds narrow tied & white fringe @ 2/3 — — — 0..17..9
To 9 y.ds Wilton Carpet — — — — @ 10/ — 4..10..0
making up of d° for 2 Tables & small carpet 1..10..0
To altering & making Carpets for Hall & Entry }
thread & binding — — — — — } 1..0..0

28th To 51 y.ds fine Cotton blue Feath for Cases of }
3 Sopha's & 76 Chair Cases — — — @ 3/10 } 9..15..6
To 152 y.ds of blue & white fringe for Chair & }
Sopha Cases — — — — @ 1/3 } 9..10..0
16½ y.ds fine blue Cotton Checks for a Sopha }
& 12 cases — — — — @ 3/3 — } 2..4..10
making 76 Chair cases blue & white fringed, tape & thread 2/ — 7..12..0

June 29 To making a Large Th: Matt: & Curled hair &c — — 2..7..6
To an other D° — — — — — 2..7..6

To a p: small Double Branch's Jan 25th smethd — 162..12..8
1..5..0
To short last — — — — — 14..7½ £ 163..17..8
Cr. By over last — — — — 14..0
7½ — 7½
:7½ 163..18..3½

Brussels carpet *c.* 1810 from the floor of the Jarvis coach. Although badly worn, enough of the 27-inch-wide pattern is visible to give an indication of the large-scale pattern in olive-green, brown, cream and gold.

Opposite:
"Men of Progress" painted by Christian Schussele includes Erastus Bigelow (standing fourth from right), inventor of the power-driven ingrain and Brussels loom. The patterned floor carpet, possibly one manufactured on his looms, is typical of the period.

probable that these descriptions of English patterns are an indication of what was also available in America. One early example of Brussels, a geometric pattern based on squares with flowers in yellows, greens, brown, cream and brick red was found in the 1788 phaeton of General L. Gansevoort of New York. Another, believed to be original carpeting, is part of the furnishing of the Jarvis coach, built about 1810.[4] It is not certain that these are the original carriage carpets, but the patterns, and the flax warp and weft, suggest an 18th- or early-19th-century date.

Other patterns of this period were described among the wares imported into New York and sold at John Brower's store. An advertisement in the *Commercial Advertiser* of 21 June 1798 offered "Carpets and Carpeting of the very best Brussels quality, to the newest landscape and other elegant patterns," as well as "Brussels and Wilton Carpeting and carpets of all sizes from 3-2 by 4 up to $6\frac{3}{4}$ by $7\frac{1}{2}$ yds."[5] In 1799, "Striped Brussels carpeting for stairs and Entries" were for sale in New York at the Norwood carpet store.[6]

Advertisements for carpet and a matching border often appear throughout the second half of the 18th century. Benjamin Franklin purchased carpeting in England in 1758, which was to be sewn together so the pattern matched, and

Opposite:
Hand-knotted English Axminster carpet *c.* 1820 imitating a fashionable Turkish pattern. Axminster patterns were often coarser than the genuine Turkish knotted carpets, because Axminsters had fewer knots per square inch.

The British portrait "a Gentleman at Breakfast" by Henry Walton, *c.* 1775–80, carefully records one contemporary fashion in floor coverings—a boldly patterned bordered wall-to-wall carpet.

Detail of two miters in the border of a mid-19th-century tapestry carpet. Often numerous miters were necessary to make a carpet fit exactly around door frames, hearths, and odd corners of the room.

which was to have a matching border.[7] Un- or mismatched patterns may have been a common occurrence with these goods. In the 1770s another advertisement claimed "likewise a beautiful piece of floor carpeting with border suitable."[8] The borders were stitched by hand to the body of the carpet, and mitered at the corners.

New materials and new inventions improved the manufacture of carpets during the late 18th and early 19th centuries. Indian jute, a strong, inexpensive bast fiber, was first imported into England in the mid-1790s and thereafter in ever-increasing quantities. It proved to be a satisfactory substitute for flax and was used for the weft and stuffers. By the late 1820s it was becoming a major backing material for pile carpets in both England and America. It has continued to be used in vast quantities well into the third quarter of the 20th century. However, political disturbances preventing shipments from India, uncertain quantities and qualities and fluctuating prices have encouraged widespread substitution of man-made yarns in carpet-making processes.

In 1804 an attachment was perfected for controlling the numerous harnesses required by the old draw looms for creating patterned fabrics. Joseph Marie Jacquard presented the model of this invention at the Industrial Exposition in Paris in 1801 for which he won a bronze medal. This patent model was the culmination of a combination of French inventions by Bronchon, who devised the method of controlling individual cords in the harness of the loom with a series of cards punched with holes. These cards would be read when steel needles pressed against them, stopping at the card, or passing through the

Engraving showing the cutting
of a chain of Jacquard pattern
cards. Each card controls the
pattern for a single crosswise
row from selvage to selvage, and
the continuous chain of cards
contains one complete pattern
repeat.

holes. Vaucanson devised a squared cylinder mechanism around which the
chain of cards was placed. The needles, reading the cards, transferred the
pattern via hooks to the harness cords. The Jacquard was adapted to carpet
manufacture within a short time, and was already in use in Philadelphia in
about 1825 for making ingrains (see pages 75–6) and became indispensable for
making Brussels. However, even with the Jacquard attachment, all carpets were
still woven by hand, and pile carpets continued to be so until the early 1850s.

The same spirit of invention and desire for economy that adapted jute and
the Jacquard to the manufacture of carpets were also the driving forces behind
steam power being applied to the weaving process. For generations, coach lace,
a narrow, decorative fabric with a raised, cut- or loop-pile figure and a flatwoven background, had been produced on hand looms. Only 2 to 4 inches wide,
coach lace embellished the interiors of coaches, bordering windows, doors

and seats, and somewhat later, the interiors of automobiles. Coach lace was available in monochrome, cream, green and maroon, and polychrome. The principles involved in weaving coach lace were related to those of Brussels carpet.

In 1837 Erastus Bigelow, needing funds to continue his study of medicine, invented a steam-powered coverlet loom. After discussing the feasibility of coach lace manufacture by steam power with the largest Boston distributor, Fairbanks, Loring & Company, he produced such a power loom.[9]

Shortly afterwards, Bigelow converted the ingrain loom to steam power, and then set his mind to weaving Brussels by power-operated looms. Numerous adaptations of the coach lace loom and the ingrain loom were required before a satisfactory loom had been made for the manufacture of Brussels. The loom had to be 27 inches wide, wider than the 2 to 4 inches common in coach lace, the pile had to cover the surface evenly, and pattern repeats had to be exact. His first model, completed in the mid-1840s, was not in fact put into use until 1849. In 1850, the first American steam-power woven Brussels carpets were advertised for sale. Only minor technical variations were necessary for the manufacture of Wiltons' tapestry Brussels and velvets. These American carpets, the first power-woven Brussels and Wiltons, were exhibited at the Great Exhibition in London in 1851. They arrived too late to be judged, but Bigelow was cited for merit by the committee for his entries.

> The specimens of Brussels carpeting exhibited by Mr. Bigelow are woven on a power loom invented and patented by him, and are better and more perfectly woven than any hand-loom goods that have come under the notice of the jury ... [He] has completely triumphed over the numerous obstacles that presented themselves, and succeeded in substituting steam power for manual labor in the manufacture of five-frame Brussels carpets ... The honor of this achievement ... must be awarded to a native of the United States.[10]

This power loom could produce 25 yards a day instead of 7, and, with improvements, shortly afterwards produced about 55. Brussels carpeting was still designed for, and woven in, 27- and 36-inch widths and it remained an expensive fabric. It was popular through the early 20th century, after which time it fell from favor, re-emerging once again in the 1970s, when it became known as a level-loop Wilton. For a time after the introduction of machine Brussels, many purchasers preferred quality British hand-woven carpeting to the new, machine Brussels. Even by mid-century, with the increasingly high standard of living, the demand for ingrain carpeting far surpassed that for Brussels and Wilton.

In order to reach new markets, 19th-century manufacturers were constantly seeking more efficient and inexpensive methods of making carpets. In 1832 Richard Whytock of Edinburgh, Scotland, invented a successful drum printing process for patterning worsted pile warps which saved wool. Tapestry carpets, woven in Scotland and later in England, were not manufactured in America until 1846, when John Johnson, a carpet-weaver in Newark, New Jersey, began the first limited production.[11] Until the invention of the Brussels power loom, all tapestry carpets were woven by hand. Tapestry Brussels and velvet carpets are essentially single-frame Brussels carpets in which all the color pattern warps appear on the surface. They conserved vast quantities of wool, used an unlimited color palette with extremely subtle and often jewel-like shadings, and permitted extensive freedom of design, particularly in the rendition of naturalistic flowers and foliage. The printing process was slow and expensive and the pattern was not as crisp and exact as Brussels, but it provided an elegant and economical alternative.

Numerous examples of the durable, colorfast Brussels, Wilton and tapestry carpeting from the mid-19th century onward still exist, some on floors, some as samples, some as carpet bags—the popular 19th-century form of suitcase or traveling satchel, for which any kind of carpeting could be used. These examples, together with contemporary paintings and photographs, show a mid-19th-century color palette dominated by brown, maroon and cream, with accents of red, blue and olive green. Patterns with floral motifs inspired by the rococo revival are often so big that two widths of carpet are needed for part of one repeat. There are three tapestry carpets in public collections, similar in appearance to each other, which are typical examples of the patterning and texture of these printed carpets. One is at Bayou Bend, Houston, Texas; one at the Wadsworth Atheneum, Hartford, Connecticut and a third in the Milligan House parlor from Saratoga, New York which is in the Brooklyn Museum. The bill of sale exists for this documented example. It was purchased in 1856 from a supplier who dealt in both American and imported floor coverings. A matching hearth rug with a border, incorporating flower motif and foliage, was sold "en suite" with the wall-to-wall carpet.[12]

Medallion motifs were a very popular form of decoration on tapestry velvet carpets. One exceptional example is a documented, imported carpet in the Morristown Historical Society in Morristown, New Jersey. It is in the house known as "Acorn Hall" built in 1853, where the furnishings and carpets are original. The medallion carpet in the front parlor was woven by John Crossley & Sons, Ltd., Halifax, England, and was one of their patterns exhibited in the Great Exhibition in London in 1851.

One taste-setter of the mid-19th century, Charles Eastlake, was rather outspoken on the subject of the prevailing taste and mode in furnishings in his book *Hints on Household Taste,* first compiled in 1868. Of carpeting he said: "A carpet, of which the pattern is shaded in imitation of natural objects becomes an absurdity when we remember that if it were really what it pretends to be, no one would walk on it with comfort."[13] Eastlake continued: "Large sprawling patterns, however attractive they may be in colour, should be avoided as utterly destructive of effect to the furniture which is placed on them, and above all, every description of shaded ornament should be sternly banished from our floors."[14] His suggestions for substituting simple, diapered patterns in popular prevailing tints contrasting with that of the wallpaper were gradually followed. Fortunately, fragments in these colors and patterns remain in the carpetings and on footstools and ottomans of the 1870s.

Harriet and Catherine Beecher, writing for American women in 1865, devoted an entire chapter to home decoration in their book, *American Woman's Home.* They cautioned the purchaser of a new house against the extravagant

Milligan sitting-room with the original 1856 tapestry velvet carpet and hearth rug in place. It was at floral carpets such as these that Eastlake's caustic comments were aimed.

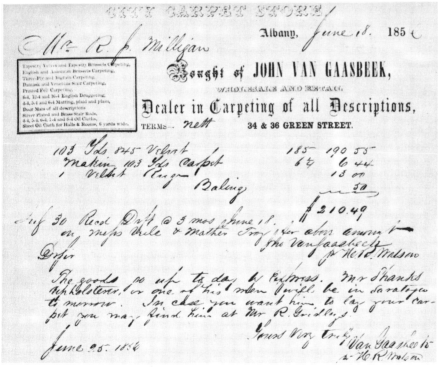

Bill dated 1856 to the R. J. Milligan household in Saratoga, New York, for supplying 103 yards sitting-room carpet, making it up, and for supplying one velvet rug.

purchase of Brussels carpet which was being sold "wonderfully cheap" because in the end it may prove to be no bargain—because of an unfashionable pattern, perhaps, or one the purchaser did not really like which, considering the wearing quality of Brussels, would outlast three or four ingrains. Instead of a bad investment in Brussels, they recommended straw matting for the parlor.[15]

Brussels and Wiltons, installed wall to wall, were taken up and cleaned, either

Sculptured surface rug in a
monochrome living-room. *c.*
1945.

professionally or out of doors, only once every couple of years. Recipes against
moths and carpet beetles were abundant, and detailed instructions for proper
sweeping and care of these valuable carpets abounded. "Not long ago [1880s],
we heard a woman say that a very stiff broom was needed for sweeping a Brussels
carpet. A carpet sweeper is the best thing for this purpose. It does the work
easily and well, and saves dust." However, if a broom of common broom-
corn was to be used instead, "it should be fine, soft, light and clean . . . Brussels
carpets are not suitable for rooms where sewing and baby-culture are going
forwards."[16] It was also recommended that, in order to sweep up threads which
may have gotten on the carpet, a broom was first dipped in clean, tepid water,
then shaken almost dry before sweeping. Dust and threads would collect on
the bristles and could then be rinsed off. The process was repeated.

Brass nails, still embedded in rectangular shapes on some late-19th-century
American floors, give mute testimony to an installation technique and possible
use of an imported pile carpet, manufactured in Scotland and Holland during
the 1880s. Such carpets were woven from a mixture of wool and jute dyed deep
maroon, and were about the thickness of Brussels. Clarence Cook, in *House
Beautiful*, said:

> A good way of using this is to make a square or parallelogram the size of the clear
> space of the floor when all the large pieces of furniture are in their places. This is
> laid down and held in its place by rings sewed to the under edge and slipped over
> small brass-headed nails, driven down close to the floor. This makes a comfortable
> footing, and is easily removed when necessary. Then in the center of the room, or
> before the fire, or in front of the sofa, lay down a bright-colored Smyrna rug.[17]

During the last quarter of the 19th century and into the early 20th, patterns
became smaller, diapered, restrained rococo foliate motifs, Persian-inspired
paisleys and eastern adaptations, in a palette of tobacco, mushroom, rust,
grayed golds and browns, combined with maroon, or off-shades of blue.
Domestic magazines and home guides were constantly urging the replacement
of wall-to-wall carpeting as floor covering by rugs for reasons of health, sanita-
tion, ease of care and longer wear. Rugs could be turned within the room and
were more economical since there was no waste as a result of fitting curious
corners of rooms. Bordered Wilton and Brussels rugs available in various sizes
were adapted to the new mode. Elaborate borders or corner motifs surrounding
central patterns of huge bunches of pink and red flowers scattered on emerald
green or black backgrounds were the height of fashion early in the 20th
century.

During the first years of this century the durable, once-prized Brussels
carpet began to disappear from American carpet showrooms and floors,
replaced by the more luxurious pile fabrics, velvets, Wiltons and Axminsters.
Floral patterns continued to be made, but during the 1920s oriental/Persian
Wilton patterns were altered to suit the taste for Chinese design prevalent at
the time. Elsie de Wolfe, decorator of the Colony Club in New York, encouraged the use of Chinese rugs, preferably imported, to be used on top of
beige and neutral solid-colored velvet carpets. Carpets again began to stretch
from wall to wall. With solid colors, seams were more apparent than on pat-

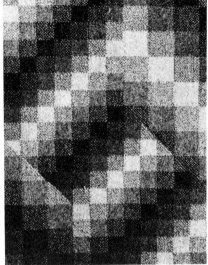

Happiness   Metropolis   Quadrangle

terned carpets, and as a result, the broad Wilton loom capable of manufacturing carpets in 12 and 15 foot widths was developed. Wool was still used for the pile, and jute for the weft. Cotton was the most common chain warp, holding the wefts in place. In the 1940s the color palette gradually changed again, to cocoa, old rose, and muted bluish greens, all colors softened with white. Sculptured surface patterns, paralleling embossed linoleums, were also features of the velvet carpets. Textured surfaces were possible by combined use of cut and looped pile, and by use of profile wires, with pattern notches cut into the upper edge of the wire to regulate the pile. Many sculptured surface textures can be obtained by this process.

Today, throughout the 1970s, only about three mills are still manufacturing woven Wilton carpets. The name Wilton has come to include the earlier Brussels construction and variations of cut, sculptured, and cut and loop textures. Wool, once the exclusive pile yarn used in these carpets, is now used only in specially ordered carpets; it is mainly replaced by nylons and synthetic blends. Even the backing, once entirely of flax, then of jute and cotton, is often made of synthetic alternatives, with qualities similar to natural fibers, but with the advantages of moisture resistance, consistent quality and availability at more stable prices. Wiltons have once again become luxury carpets, accounting for but a fraction of the total carpet output. Numerous standard styles are available at a moment's notice, others can be custom-designed in comparatively limited quantities, in materials best suited to the decor and use of the room.

Three color-coordinated patterns designed by Jack Lenor Larsen for use in a single office complex. Varied patterns and textures lend interest and definition to office spaces. *Left:* Cut-and-loop surface gives texture and emphasis to the colors. *Center:* Looped-pile Wilton with subtle change of pattern scale. *Right:* Looped-pile Wilton with recessed squares.

8 Turkey Work, Axminster and Chenille

Turkey work and Axminster carpets were 17th- and 18th-century European knotted carpet forms devised as substitutes for the rare and expensive imported Turkey carpets (for construction details see pages 76ff.). Writings, recording for example "one Turkey Carpett of Englishe Makinge" or "one foote Turky carpett,"[1] give an insight into this fashion for a hand-knotted form with a knotted wool pile and linen warp and weft; it lasted from the 17th century to the mid-18th century. Some patterns imitated imported pieces, others adapted stylized tulip, carnation and interlacing strapwork motifs, closely following embroidery designs.[2] Almost exclusively during this time, hand-knotted turkey work was used as a cover for tables, cupboards or as upholstery for chairs, and in America in the inventories and wills of the first half of the 18th century such carpets were almost always listed with a specific piece of furniture. Some 18th-century portraits demonstrate this. They depict families sitting around tables that are covered with table carpets; the patterns and colors are similar to those predominant in 17th- and 18th-century carpets from Turkey, Anatolia and the Caucasus.[3] Other portraits, painted later in the 18th century, show richly colored and patterned Turkish carpets used as floor covering as well as on tables. These carpets may well have been the prized possessions of the portrait sitter, or they may have been artists' props for the purpose of lending elegance and formality to the painting. It seems, however, that Turkish carpets were not widely used in the colonies

Knots used in hand-knotted carpets. *Left:* Turkish or Ghiordes knot, frequently found in Axminsters. Both ends of the tuft emerge from the center of a pair of warps. The end of the left-hand tuft is carried along to form the second tuft and both tufts are then cut apart. *Center and right:* Persian or Sehna knots, both left hand and right hand. With Persian knots, one end of the yarn appears between each warp. In each drawing, two knots have been made, joined by an uncut loop of yarn.

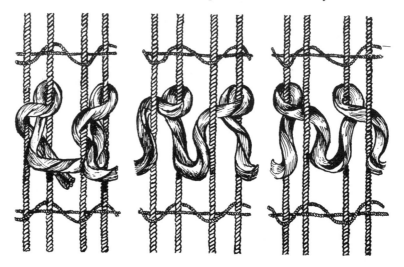

"Old '76 and Young '48" painted by Richard Caton Woodville, 1849. Oriental-pattern floor coverings were not the height of fashion in the mid-19th century, but these patterns continued in painted floors, floorcloths or Turkish carpeting. Here the carpet is protected by one of the most common floor coverings in the 19th century—a hearth rug.

until after the mid-18th century. In 1766, John Wayles of Virginia, writing to merchants in Bristol, England, commented that "In 1740 I don't remember to have seen such a thing as a turkey Carpet in the Country except a small thing in a bed chamber. Now, nothing are so common as Turkey or Wilton Carpetts, the whole Furniture of the Roomes Elegant and every appearance of Opulence."[4]

By the second half of the 18th century they were available in large sizes— $11\frac{1}{2}$ feet by $18\frac{1}{2}$ feet or 22 feet by 15 feet. Smaller ones were also available. There was a report of a "Turkey Carpet of various colours, about a yard and half in length, and a Yard wide, fringed on each end," which had been stolen and commanded a $3.00 reward.[5] They were for sale at auction, as part of "the genteel House Furniture" or available by import.[6] Wealthy Americans would go to England to choose their carpets personally as did Benjamin Franklin when he was in London in 1765. At the written request of his wife, Deborah, he chose "a Large True Turkey Carpet cost 10 Guineas, for the Dining Parlour."[7] Those unable to choose one themselves gave specific instructions to their purchasing agents in London so a suitable one could be sent.

By the late 18th century, however, Turkish carpets seem to have become less fashionable, giving in to the Brussels, Wiltons and ingrains, styles increasingly used throughout the 19th century. Not until the 1880s was there again a widespread revival of oriental carpets as fashionable floor-covering.

Overleaf:
The clear, precise patterning and rich colors which go through to the backing in this 1977 adaptation of a Navajo rug have been made possible by radical new printing methods specially adapted for printing pile surfaces.

Opposite:
American Oriental rug and runner, 1977. The pattern has been in continuous production on Karastan's spool Axminster looms since 1927. These Axminster rugs, with a soft, flexible structure allowing them to be folded in either direction, closely resemble the oriental carpets from which they were copied.

Clarence Cook, in his wonderful book on interior decoration, *What Shall We Do With Our Walls?*, in 1880 commented:

> The things that go to the furnishing of a house are so vastly improved with us, and things once rare are now become so common—either the things themselves, or their faithful copies—that it is a comparatively easy matter, not even calling for much money, for people in ordinarily good circumstances to have their rooms looking, not merely comfortable, but handsome. Carpets have always been the rule in American houses, but then Eastern rugs were long scarce, or wholly unknown; now, however, they are to be had in abundance, even good ones are within easy reach, and those the connoisseur calls poor are, many of them, not to be despised.[8]

After considerable disagreement by the authors of the domestic encyclopedias on merits of room-sized rugs versus wall-to-wall carpeting, rugs gradually began to gain favor during the 1870s. About this time too, wealthy leaders of transportation, finance and industry began building luxurious, elegant residences in major cities—Boston, New York, Chicago, Cincinnati—and furnished them with the finest, most fashionable items money could buy, including countless oriental carpets spread layer upon layer on extravagant parquet floors, in parlors, dining rooms, hallways and studies.

In the 1890s two immigrant brothers, Arshag and Miran Karagheusian, born in Constantinople, established an importing business in America. At first they imported textiles, then mocca and sesame seeds. A desire to improve their business, a widespread demand for oriental rugs, and their own background encouraged them to begin importing oriental carpets. Not only did they buy directly from the merchants in the bazaars, but they also designed rugs, planning the colors to be made by hand in the near-eastern rug "factories."[9]

By 1903 oriental patterns were woven on American Wilton and Axminster machines, produced in an enormous variety of sizes, colors and patterns. Department stores such as W. & J. Sloane and John Wanamaker displayed rugs in showrooms decorated in the Persian bazaar manner—rug on rug, pattern on pattern—so fashionable in elegant houses.

Gradually, once again the fashion changed, and during the 1920s floor coverings of Chinese origin or inspiration were the rage. The Karagheusians were among the major importers of oriental carpets, including hand-knotted Chinese rugs. Another merchant, Mrs. H. B. Merrick of Ann Arbor, Michigan, operated a store there, Merrick's Heirloom Rugs, which specialized in designing and importing hand made Chinese rugs. If a customer wished, she would create a custom design rug from various patterns listed in her catalogue. It was a little like choosing from a Chinese menu, with column A and column B. Among the choices were art rugs, with a sehna knotted handspun wool pile; lustrous rugs of machine spun yarns which had a chemically produced antique luster, and hooked rugs, which used only wool yarns for the pile. Designs included Jewel tree, Chinese symbols, beveled, brocade flowers, plain, stenciled dragons, with or without border. The customer could choose the combination that appealed most to his personal taste, and then Mrs. Merrick would send the designs to be manufactured by the Jen-li Company, which had branches in Peking and Tientsin.[10]

These rugs were romantic, personal, and expensive—more expensive than those of domestic manufacture. The demand for Chinese carpets abated in

Well-appointed stair-hall library recorded by the photographer, Byron, in 1898. Oriental rugs in many different patterns and sizes cover floors, stairs and table.

Fine Oriental carpets for sale at the S.E. Olson Company, Minneapolis, Minnesota, as advertised in the *Dry Goods Economist*, 1918. A "Turkish Bazaar" was a popular carpet display technique at that time.

Weavers working at a mid-19th-century vertical carpet loom, probably similar to that used by Whitty in the 18th century to manufacture hand-knotted Axminsters.

the early 1930s to the extent that patterns were no longer imitated in Wiltons, hooked rugs and linoleum.

Even during the 1940s, '50s and early '60s, when solid-colored carpets were more widely used, and many oriental carpets were rolled up in attics, a brisk trade in orientals in Boston, Pittsburgh and Baltimore continued. Turkish and Persian carpets—antique, semi-antique and modern—as well as carved surface Chinese rugs, which, with the reinstatement of trade, have become available once again, enjoy popularity along with a wide variety of area rugs in American homes today.

During the late 19th century and throughout the 20th, domestic and imported rugs with oriental patterns in both hand-knotted and power loom construction have lain side-by-side on the floors in American homes, creating and providing for an ever widening market. Even today, centuries after the first oriental carpets were imported into the colonies, hand-knotted imported oriental carpets are still eagerly sought. Machine-woven Axminster was developed in the 1870s to resemble closely the hand-woven product.

Hand-knotted carpets, of any origin, were a luxurious and extravagant commodity and, during the 17th and 18th centuries, the majority came from the Near East. In an attempt to provide a more economical alternative, an English weaver named Parisot obtained royal patronage in the 1750s for the manufacture of hand-knotted floor carpets on a vertical broadloom such as was in use in France. Although there was widespread interest in these carpets, in 1755 the venture failed.

However, before it did, a weaver from Axminster, Thomas Whitty, visited the factory. His curiosity had been aroused by seeing a newly imported Turkish carpet, 36 feet by 21 feet and seamless. "I had some little knowledge of figure weaving," he wrote, "but could not conceive by what means a carpet of so great a breadth could be woven in a figure without a seam in it."[11] He worked out a tiny knotted sample on his loom, and saw, at the London factory of Parisot, large seamless carpets being made on vertical looms. Whitty adopted this procedure.[12]

In 1756, a year after the Parisot factory failed, the Royal Society of Arts offered a monetary prize for the best hand-knotted wool pile carpet as an incentive for the new carpet knotting industry. The competition required that the carpets be large, at least 12 feet by 15 feet, and "made after the fashion of the Turkish ones."[13] Thomas Whitty and Thomas Moore of Moorfields were the first contenders for the prize. One provided a product of better materials, the other at a better price, so the prize was shared. The following year, Whitty shared the prize again, this time with Claude Passavant, a weaver from Exeter. The third year, submitting six superior carpets, Whitty won the entire prize. Although the carpets continued to be made in several towns, they became known generically as "Axminsters." Not all the carpets, however, copied Turkish patterns. Many incorporated formal medallion floral and arabesque motifs, which reflected the decorative ceiling and furniture designs created by Robert Adam and others in the late 18th century.

By the 1790s some Axminster carpets were being manufactured in the United States as well. William Peter Sprague, proprietor of one of the earliest recorded

Floral Axminster carpet, *c.* 1785, at Colonial Williamsburg, Virginia. Naturalistic floral and foliate motifs were easily produced by the hand-knotted Axminster technique. Rugs similar to this one appeared in several late-18th-century paintings such as the one below.

"Mrs Congreve & Family" painted by P. Reinagle. Carpet similar in pattern and style to the 1785 floral Axminster carpet above.

Staff of Independence National Historic Park putting finishing touches to the rendering for the reconstruction of the 18th-century carpet which was originally designed by Sprague for the Senate Chamber. A graph pattern will be made from the rendering, and the carpet, approximately 20 feet by 40 feet, will be hand knotted.

American carpet factories in the United States, was trained in Axminster manufacture in England, and was making carpets of "those durable kind called Turkey and Axminster" by 1791. Account book records show that George Washington purchased dining-room carpeting from Sprague in 1791, and in the same year he was commissioned to weave the carpet for the Senate Chamber in Congress Hall, Philadelphia. Unlike the English ones, his were woven 27 inches wide. *The New York Magazine or Literary Repository* for June 1791 described the carpet in detail:

The device wove in the last mentioned, is the Crest and Armorial Atchievements [*sic*] appertaining to the United States. Thirteen Stars forming a constellation, diverging from a cloud, occupy the space under the chair of the Vice-President. The AMERICAN EAGLE is displayed in the centre, holding in his dexter talon an olive branch, in his sinister a bundle of thirteen arrows, and in his beak, a scroll inscribed with the motto E pluribus unum. The whole surrounded by a chain formed of 13 shields, emblematic of each state.

The sides are ornamented with marine and land trophies, and the corners exhibit very beautiful Corn Copias [*sic*], some filled with olive branches and flowers expressive of peace, while others bear fruit and grain, the emblems of plenty.

Under the arms, on the pole which supports the cap of liberty, is hung the balance of justice.

The whole being executed in capital stile, with rich bright colours has a very fine effect, notwithstanding the raw materials employed, and of the refuse and coarser kind; that this manufactory is an advantage to others by allowing a price for the articles which could not be used in the common branches of woolen and tow business.[14]

This description was very specific and the emblems and motifs were well understood by 18th-century readers. From account book records of yardage and cost, the period description, and comparison of proportions and motifs from pattern books and other period Axminster carpets, John Milley, Supervisory Curator of the Independence National Historic Park, along with the staff, have been able to recreate Sprague's carpet design which will be hand-knotted and reinstalled in the Senate Chamber.

Axminsters continued to be manufactured in America. In 1832 American production of Axminsters, at the Lowell Manufacturing Company, Lowell, Massachusetts, was very limited—less than 2,000 rugs per year.[15] Limited quantities of hand-knotted Axminster also known at that time in America as moquette were woven throughout the 1840s in New England mills.

Moquette was a type of woven, tufted carpet resembling velvet. Its name derived from the French 18th-century carpet known as Moquette, made by a painfully slow hand process which would take two weavers and one boy an entire day to produce $1\frac{1}{2}$ yards of carpeting. Moquette, however, was also an American machine-made pile carpet. In the 1870s it was introduced as a less expensive power-woven substitute for imported Axminsters "which had long been beyond the reach of the average housekeeper's purse. In America, it sprang into immediate popularity."[16]

The pile of moquette was longer and thicker than the popular tapestry and Wilton carpets. It was manufactured by a process designed to duplicate the individually inserted and colored tufts of Axminster, invented in 1865 by Halcyon Skinner, while he was working for the Alexander Smith & Sons Carpet Company of Yonkers, New York. Numerous improvements were made, and by the mid-1870s elaborate patterns, containing as many as 50 colors, were being woven at the rate of 40 to 60 yards per day. "Axminster Moquettes" were manufactured by Alexander Smith & Sons Company, and by the Hartford Carpet Company. By the late 19th century, these carpets were almost always available with matching hall and stair carpets. They were the "acme of perfection from a colorist's standpoint . . . softly shaded in colors, toned low and aesthetic, nothing bright or striking. Designs are floral or geometrical; colors mostly light, construction [of rugs] same as carpet . . . they are very heavy."[17]

Pictorial rugs were a very popular type of floor covering from about 1895 until the teens. Their wide range of patterns developed from the versatility of Axminster construction. The basic construction was adapted slightly by

Popular Axminster rug *c.* 1910–14 variously known as Bigelow Axminster or Hartford Bussorah picture rug.

All-wool Axminster of the early
1950s with an all-over flower
pattern in subtle, shaded, pastel
flower tones set against a
delicate beige ground.

Opposite:
This sculptured wall tapestry
with a motif based on
midwestern landscapes was
made by Edward Fields, Inc.
and designed for use as dividers
in American Airlines 727 wide
body planes.

Overleaf:
Custom hand-tufted rugs in
process at the V'Soske workshop
in Puerto Rico.

Marshall Field & Company, which set up an Axminster mill in North Carolina
to manufacture oriental patterned carpets now known as Karastan. These
carpets, with patterns recreated from antique orientals, do not have the stiff
construction characteristic of Axminsters. Instead, the colors of the surface,
not hidden by weft and stuffers, can be seen on the back, and the carpet can be
folded in either direction. They are also specially washed and buffed to give
an antique sheen—a process not applied to standard Axminsters.

Until the 1950s, Axminsters were widely used in America. They are still
manufactured by a few mills, but in limited quantities, their once popular
and prestigious position usurped by new types of carpeting in monochrome,
tweed or textured, unpatterned surfaces.

Throughout the 19th century, carpet manufacturers continuously sought
new ways to produce carpets faster and more economically. The Chenille-
Axminster process was developed in Glasgow, Scotland, by James Templeton
in 1839 to produce rugs which could compete with the wide, seamless, expensive Axminsters. It was a double loom process. Any pattern could be produced,
in any required shape—as a rug, or to fit a difficult room shape. It only became
popular in America after World War I. Kendrick wrote in 1922 that "the

manufacture of chenille floor coverings is really an infant industry in this country. About thirty years ago, some effort was made to get into this business in America, but unfavorable tariff legislation discouraged it."[18] Nevertheless, there are instances of chenille carpets or patent Axminsters imported into the United States. "The Americans are extensive buyers," commented the *Carpet Trade* in 1876, "but it is necessary to design patterns and employ colours for them such as would find no sale in the English market, the former gigantic in size, and sometimes grotesque, and the latter of the most glowing and extraordinary tints; pretentious and vulgar, with figures of animals and other incongruous elements. Messrs. Templeton have recently supplied one of this character, measuring 42 by 41 feet, for an hotel at San Francisco."[19]

A purely American variation of chenille was a heavy, reversible, tufted fabric frequently patterned, referred to as "Smyrna." It could be made in sizes from door mats to 15 feet wide and although it was, perhaps, a "cheap outgrowth" of the Chenille-Axminsters produced in Scotland, it had become "among the most desirable of American coverings . . . It is not extravagant to claim it not only as a distinctive American weave, but also as a Philadelphia weave."[20]

Smyrna carpets were also woven by a two-step (double-loom) process, the chenille wefts being twisted to provide a pile surface on both sides. During the 1890s, floral or geometrical patterns, or those which included lions, dogs, and peacocks, were prevalent. Colors were soft and subdued, or bright and attractive, as desired.[21] By the 1920s, the vogue for these fringed double-sided pile rugs had passed.

Perhaps Elsie de Wolfe was describing a chenille floor covering when she wrote "Everything else (except for the blue and white chintz) in the room was white except the thick cream rug with its border of blue and rose and buff, and the candlesticks and appliqués which repeated the colors."[22]

Chenille's wide-loom construction made it particularly suitable for providing, during the 1930s and '40s, seamless carpets up to 20 feet in width—wall-to-wall sizes in single and two-tone colors for houses, and in patterns for large spaces in public buildings. Perhaps, of all the machine manufactured carpeting, chenille comes closest to custom carpeting, since it required extensive hand work, and could be designed and woven to fit any space with a minimum of waste, covering the floor with a deep, luxurious pile.

Cost limited the use of chenille during the 1920s and '30s and its slow, comparatively archaic manufacturing process soon made it fall by the wayside. Countless technological advances and adaptations made possible chenille, moquette, Smyrna and Axminster as carpet types and as alternatives to the hand-knotted carpets of the East. Even though the machine Axminster process closely imitated the desired effect, carpet technology still has not mastered the art of tying knots in the subtle intricate eastern patterns so adeptly produced by hand.

Overleaf:
English cross-stitch embroidered rug *c.* 1750. The formal stylized flowers and border motifs are characteristic of these elegant, costly floor coverings which are the product of domestic leisure or atelier commissions.

Opposite:
Detail of a Victorian cross-stitch embroidered carpet *c.* 1860 in a popular motif of the mid-19th century. Similar dog patterns appear in period needlework guides and in Edward Frost's catalogues for hooked rugs.

Plain walls, simple furnishings and solid-colored carpets introduced by Elsie de Wolfe in 1898 influenced the search for wider looms to produce solid-colored seamless carpeting. Compare with the well-appointed stair-hall library at the turn of the century, on page 131.

9 Tufted Carpets

Tufted carpets were a new type of floor covering which evolved out of a particular early American hand-embroidery technique known as candlewick embroidery; they developed into a major 20th-century industry. The evolution of the technique took a long time.

Candlewick bedspreads were very popular during the late 18th and early 19th centuries, and were made in the following way: several strands of candlewicking were used as a sewing thread stitched into a cotton or linen fabric. The pattern was formed with embroidery stitches—french knots, stem and chain stitches, or a loose running stitch which left loops of wicking on the top surface; the running stitches were then clipped to form small tufts. Usually

White-on-white candlewick bedspread worked by Alida Holmes of Montgomery County, New York, in 1812.

the patterns were linear with leaves, centers or flower petals solidly embroidered. They were usually, in addition, entirely white on white. After the embroidery had been completed, the coverlets were laundered in very hot water to shrink the fabric, the tufts being held tightly in place which prevented pulling out and caused them to untwist and become fluffier.

This type of bedcovering disappeared from fashionable households throughout the second half of the 19th century, to be, in a sense, rediscovered by Catherine Evans Whitener of Dalton, Georgia, who, in 1895, made a hand-tufted bedspread as a wedding present. As other people heard of this bedspread, and demand for them grew, she made more to sell, and, in turn, also taught neighbors how to make them. Soon many of these spreads were being made in the area surrounding Dalton, often from materials brought in by a supplier who collected the finished spreads to sell—a cottage industry procedure reminiscent of the early carpet mills in Philadelphia in the 18th century. Colors were no longer just white on white, but there were also white tufts on colored backgrounds, and colored tufts, in patterns with names reminiscent of the beloved quilting patterns: "Square Circle," "Wedding Ring," "Wild Rose."

By the 1920s "Chenille" fabrics became synonymous with the term candle-wicking to describe tufted bathmats, beach robes and bedspreads. With such a popular demand for these items, it was not long before a method was devised

Tufted bathmat *c.* 1930 of pale sage green with peach-colored flowers. It was probably one of the earliest single needle tufted floor coverings having both backing and pile of cotton.

to mechanize the industry for faster, less expensive production.

It may well have been the characteristic row of loops left along the stitching line of an improperly threaded sewing machine, or one which had incorrect tension, which first suggested that tufting could be done on a sewing-machine. During the 1930s a commercial sewing-machine was adapted for tufting by incorporating a needle with an eye large enough to carry the tufting yarns, and a knife blade/looper to replace the bobbin. With this machine, the tufted surface was always produced on the underside. A logical development of this was a needle bar containing multiple needles. The first tufted floor coverings to be made with single-needle machines or with narrow multiple-needle machines were scatter rugs and bath mats. However, when seamed, these narrow widths did not produce a very elegant product.

Not until after World War II did the broadloom tufting machines begin to revolutionize the carpet industry.[1] Many small mill operations sprang up in garages in Georgia, in cement-block buildings with one tin wall for ease of expansion. Many of these tiny mills, operating with very little capital, had only one tufting machine. Some parts of the process, such as dying and finishing, were jobbed out. As with the tiny weaving mills in the early 19th century, many 20th-century proprietors joined the ranks to provide tufted carpet to fulfil the American dream of carpeted floors, a dream spurred on by a building boom of residential and commercial structures after World War II and the Korean War. Many of the established weaving mills set up tufting divisions to compete with this less expensive, rapidly produced carpet.[2] Today, several hundred manufacturers are involved in the manufacture of tufted carpets. (For construction details, see page 83.) But gradually, just as in the mid-19th century, new industry giants are emerging—among them Barwick, Coronet, World, Horizon, Milliken.

The combined effect of new, expanding markets, carpets produced with synthetic yarns and backings whose quality and texture could be more closely controlled than natural fibers, increasingly sophisticated computer-controlled patterns, and new dyeing and finishing processes, led to new concepts in the pattern, texture and surface of carpeting. The shag carpet, a speciality of Californian rug mills during the late 1950s and early '60s, was an example of this. It had a long, deep pile which stood $\frac{3}{4}$ inch or more long and required a special "shag rake" to groom it. This fashionable floor covering available in myriad colors—orange, lime green, electric blues in solids and tweeds— rapidly spread through the United States. The new dyeing and printing processes provided a large variety of textures and shades, some designed to resemble the subtle shading on solid-colored velvet carpets. These patterning processes are far more satisfactory on plush or "splush" carpets, with dense, resilient cut pile, closely resembling the former Wilton, Axminster and chenille carpets, than on shag.

Numerous processes have been developed including yarns with varying dye absorption properties, tac dye and screen printing. The most radical new machine to date, completely controlled by computer, is the Millitron process, invented by Dr. William Stewart for the Deering Milliken Company. By adapting existing computer technology, a five-color printing process has been developed which controls minute quantities of color. These fine jets of color are forced through the entire depth of the cut pile and into the backing. By careful programming of color overlays, far more than the original number of colors can be produced. Likewise, with the flick of a dial, radically different patterns programmed within the same color palette can be obtained, as well as rugs of different sizes, from a door mat to a rug 12 feet by 15 feet. Although this process can be used for broadloom, most of the finished carpeting is made

Two-level cut-and-loop shag-tufted carpet in a popular overall tweed pattern, *c.* 1975.

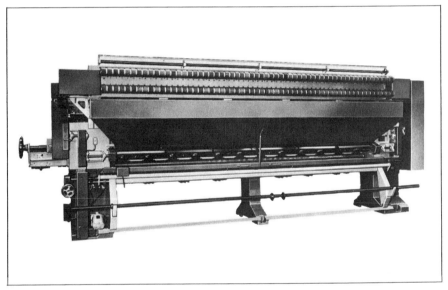

Tufting machine.

into rugs, to be used on floors, on walls, perhaps, even on tables.

Dan Stark, a leading designer of Millitron process carpets, commented that the future trend of American floor covering lies in the direction of the widespread use of low-level-loop wall-to-wall carpeting, resilient vinyl floorings, or wall-to-wall mattings, any of which give a permanent underfoot surface on which rugs provide a color accent and can easily be transported to another room or elsewhere. Although the return to the 18th- and 19th-century fashion for rugs is not yet complete, rugs are nevertheless providing an ever greater choice for the American consumer, used alone, or paired with tufted broadloom carpetings.

Tufting machines not only produce cut-pile broadlooms but also such effects as multilevel loops, where the pile is of varying heights either because of programmed tension variations, or special yarn properties which cause greater or lesser shrinkage when finishing processes are applied. Some patterns and

Cut-pile, tufted carpet with a printed pattern, adapted from an Indian motif.

textures are created by using combinations of cut and looped pile, sometimes on a single level, sometimes a multi-level. In order to produce a denser pile—one which does not separate in straight stitching lines—the machines were adapted to include a step-over, a control in which the primary backing (the fabric into which the pile is stitched) moves forward under the needles in a zig-zag or "S" pattern.

Originally a cotton primary backing was used on all tufted carpets—later jute and man-made woven and non-woven substitutes were used. Latex, applied to the back of the primary backing, both holds the tufts in place and acts as a bonding agent to hold the secondary backing. This second backing is necessary to provide a more substantial weight and body, and increase the dimensional stability of the carpet, which, without this latex and second backing, would have the feel of a one-sided bathtowel. Very often carpets, primary and secondary backings, as well as pile, are made from materials impervious to moisture, molds, mildew, sunbleaching and moths. This has played a large part in opening up new carpeting markets. With such properties carpets can be designed for kitchens and bathrooms, patios and porches, baseball fields and apartment "gardens," grass strips and median dividers on

Wall-to-wall carpeting blends floor, steps and furniture together. New, permanent-installation techniques on floors and stairs have eliminated the need for stair rods. A decorative rope conceals the seam.

Deep-pile tufted rug used in a dining-room in 1977. Ease of care, and improved vacuum cleaners and cleaning products, have made obsolete the use of crumbcloths and floorcloths as protective coverings.

highways.[3] Frequently referred to as "Astro Turf," this bright green grassy material is an adaptation of pile carpeting using modern materials and technology to provide an easy-care, bug-proof substitute for the more expensive or slower growing commodity.

Needlepunch carpet, also known as needle-bonded or needle-loomed, is a type of felted, flat-surface carpet, closely resembling the felted hair matting used as padding under carpets. Such a carpet, with its flat, fairly smooth surface, is well adapted to screen-printed patterns. Impervious to moisture and exceptionally light in weight, it too, can be used indoors or out.

Machine-knitted carpets with a pile surface may well be considered the ultimate sophisticated adaptation of the mid-19th-century shaggy rugs. They are currently manufactured in the United States and provide another modern carpet option.

Tufted carpets have radically changed the carpet industry within a mere 30 years. By the mid-1970s tufted carpeting, accounting for nearly 95 per cent of the total carpets produced in the United States, had reached undreamed-of proportions. The combination of innovative technology and vast supplies of synthetic fibers made the product within the reach of millions of Americans.[4]

10 Embroidered Carpets

Eighteenth-century journals, advertisements and order books contain barely a reference to the sale of English needleworked rugs, whereas references to Brussels, Wilton, ingrain and list carpets are abundant. Embroidered carpets were a luxurious commodity, requiring vast quantities of wool and canvas. They were made for domestic use in England, not for export, and were owned by wealthy English families, some of whom can be identified from coats of arms worked into the carpet.[1] If they had been available for sale in America we could expect recorded evidence of their use in wealthy American homes.

One of the very few references to such a carpet appeared in 1802. A carpet with characteristics of the English embroidered form, with formal, stylized floral and border patterns worked in canvas embroidery stitches on linen, was offered for sale in Charleston, South Carolina: "An elegant broad cloth carpet wrought with different kinds of fruits and flowers, to be seen at the subscriber's house, No. 35 Queen Street. Price, One Hundred Guineas."[2] There can be speculation about the origin and construction of this carpet, but the description

Formal, English embroidered carpet, 1740–65, in which the entire pattern is worked in cross stitch.

offers certain clues. "Wrought," a term generally associated with needlework, suggests embroidery; "elegant" suggests a refinement of style in the "Fruits and Flowers" in the pattern. It was being sold in Charleston, a southern seaport in which quantities of English goods were traded. If indeed it was an English embroidered carpet, it was probably one of the very few which were in America, even though by now many fine examples are in American museum collections.[3] There is a remote chance that this "wrought" carpet was an unidentified American embroidered floor carpet but, in view of the lack of a tradition of embroidered floor carpets in 18th-century America to parallel that in England, either in type or style, this seems unlikely. It may, however, have been a bed rug.

Bed rugs, the predecessor of the later yarn-sewn hearth rugs, were an American embroidery form, equally luxurious and elegant as their English floor counterparts. They were used as warm, decorative coverings for beds, and were made in the lush Connecticut River Valley and other established New England communities, mainly in towns founded in the early 17th century —Ipswich, Massachusetts (1633); Andover, Massachusetts (1643); Torrington, Connecticut (c. 1735); Hartford, Connecticut (c. 1735); Flushing, New York (1635).[4]

This was a region of enormous wealth, of long-established towns with large houses, vast acres of fertile farmlands; a region in which, by the early 18th century, settlers had more raw materials than were necessary for survival, and they had the time to use them creatively. They could afford new homespun wool, dyed in sufficient quantities to embroider an elaborate overall pile-surface pattern on a large bed covering. They could afford to use a quality woven blanket as a backing. The patterns—reflecting the fashion of the time—

American bed rug, worked entirely in stem stitch during the last quarter of the 18th century by Hannah Pearl who lived in the Pomfret-Hampton area of Connecticut. The bold stylized motifs, openness and freedom of patterning distinguish these bed rugs from their English counterparts.

Cross-section of cut-and-looped
yarn-sewn rug. The backing
fabric can be seen between the
stitches which show on the back
of the rug. This is one of the
identifying characteristics of
embroidered rugs.

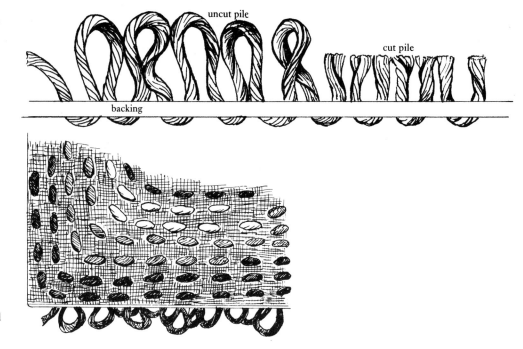

Reverse side of a cut-and-looped
yarn-sewn rug.

were boldly and heavily embroidered with fruits and flowers into a purely
American form, distinguished by the materials and methods used in their
construction. About forty of these bed rugs, most initialled and dated—the
earliest in 1722—span more than a century. They traced an American decorative tradition and provided the model for the late-18th-century floor covering,
the hearth rug, which adapted the materials and construction for use on the
floor.

Now known as yarn sewn rugs, these small, early American floor coverings
were worked on a linen background in looped, running stitches in homespun
wools, or in wool-saving crewel stitches also used on bed hangings and petticoat
borders. They were made to be used perhaps as bedside rugs, as hearth rugs
to provide some warmth or color in a parlor, or as protection for a woven carpet
(if the family was fortunate enough to own one). By the 1790s, hearth rugs were
available for sale, offered by merchants in newspapers and advertisements.
One such "fire rug" protected the fine Brussels carpet in the presidential
mansion of Thomas Jefferson in the first decade of the 19th century.[5]

About the same time, a distinction began to be made in contemporary
dictionaries between rugs for beds, and rugs for use on the floor. Some rugs
were woven for specific use as hearth rugs, and yarn sewn rugs, with their
bordered floral patterns, genre scenes of houses, animals, trees, geometric and
nautical motifs, reminiscent of samplers, were adaptations of the fashionable
woven floor coverings.

Like bed rugs, yarn-sewn rugs seem to have been a New England form,
perhaps worked at home, perhaps the product of the schoolgirl's art, just as
were many of the other embroidery forms of the early 19th century. In 1810
an advertisement offered "instruction in . . . tambour, embroidery, rugs and
other worsted work . . . at the Boarding and Day School" of Mrs. Davis in

Boston.[6] The instruction she offered for rug making might have meant yarn-sewn rugs, although it could also have indicated the craze for Berlin wool embroidery and raised scissor-sculptured pile which was a form of worsted work.[7] Yarn-sewn rugs are believed to have been worked between 1790 and about 1850. A stair runner from Goshen, New York, made by Caroline Norton and dated 1842 is probably one of the latest of the 19th-century examples. Unlike bed rugs, few yarn-sewn rugs have been signed and still fewer have been dated. Until recently they were thought to have been hooked rugs, since, when seen from the cut or looped pile surface, they look very much like hooked rugs. They seem to have been a transitional form of floor covering which ultimately led to hooked rugs—one which sometimes used only homespun wools stitched through the backing; sometimes combining these with other kinds of pile such as shirred rags. On the whole they make use of a variety of available materials to produce a finished rug. This form seems to have died out with the widespread availability of burlap for rug hooking.

With increased wealth, plenty of raw materials, and the luxury of conspicuous leisure among the wealthy during the 19th century, large embroidered rugs on canvas using new wools in cross stitch as well as other canvas embroidery stitches were made. But even these American embroidered carpets were suffi-

Needlework rug made by Anna Baker as a schoolgirl, during the first quarter of the 19th century; in Bakersfield, Vermont.

Detail of an early-19th-century yarn-sewn rug and its reverse side. It is worked in a variety of yarn-saving embroidery stitches.

The Pliney Moore Carpet, made
in Champlain, New York, was
finished in 1812. Its large size,
latticework center, and sea-shell
motif border—adapted from a
handkerchief—and new
materials, made it quite unusual
for the time.

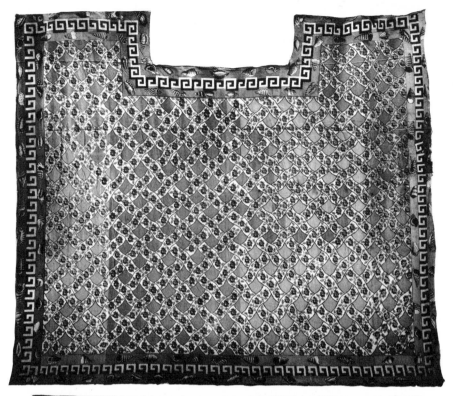

The floral, animal and foliate
patterned squares which make
up the Caswell carpet are among
the most familiar of any
American embroidered carpet.

ciently rare to be referred to by the name of their owner or maker. One example, 18 feet by 15 feet 8 inches, known as the Pliney Moore carpet, was finished in 1812. It was begun in 1808 in Champlain, New York, by Martha Corbin Moore and her daughters, Ann and Sophia, to provide an elegant carpet which could be produced from nearby available materials "since at that time, no woven carpets were brought as far North as Canada."[8] They used as a backing linen canvas brought from Montreal and wools from their own sheep, which they spun and dyed. The entire rug, shaped to fit around the hearthstone, was worked in cross stitches. A separate, bordered hearth rug embroidered with a central motif of deer and hounds protected the carpet in winter and covered the hearth in summer.

Another early rug, possibly the best known, is the Caswell carpet, which was started in 1835 by Zeruah Higley Guernsey of Castelton, Vermont. According to legend, it was embroidered on a tambour frame with a wooden hook. Each of the 76 squares is embroidered with a different pattern: stylized flowers and foliage, patterns which resemble quilt designs, and a man and lady in period dress. There are even several squares with cats and puppies cavorting on striped rugs, which could perhaps be the familiar rag or Venetian carpeting of the 19th century. This large parlor rug, shaped to fit around the edge of the hearth, has a separate hearth rug embroidered with a large basket of flowers and bordered with a red saw-tooth pattern.[9] Another 19th-century carpet was made of yarns salvaged from socks and other worn knitted goods. The

One of the few remaining pieces of the magnificent embroidered carpet which was submitted by Mrs E. G. Minor to the New York State Fair in 1844.

pattern was drawn in charcoal on bagging canvas and worked in tambour stitching into a rug 16 feet square. It was completed by Mrs. E. G. Minor in 1844 after nearly eight years' work and submitted to the state fair needlework competition. Arriving too late to be included, this spectacular Victorian pictorial carpet was given special exhibition space. Eventually the rug was divided among family members. Although only a few of the pictorial sections have been recorded, some included medieval horsemen chasing an ox, two pheasants in a forest, sheep and shepherds, bouquets and vases of flowers surrounded by leaves—patterns similar to some of the hooked rugs from the same period. [10]

A chain-stitched carpet, as well as many of the other embroidered types, required an embroidery frame or hoop to keep the fabric tight while it was being worked. Probably most of the small embroidered hearth rugs of the 19th century were worked on an adjustable embroidery frame like the one in the illustration on this page.

In her 1859 *Ladies' Hand Book of Fancy and Ornamental Work* Miss Florence Hartley, describing the best approach for worsted work embroidery, writes:

> The pattern best adapted to this kind of work is such as is given in the design, in which a skilful arrangement of geometrical figures almost makes the pattern. The Principle of the pattern is visible, especially in Eastern work, such as Turkey and Persian carpets, and cashmere shawls—thick, close patterns, strongly contrasted in color, so small in the details that nothing but the general effect is apprehended by the eye, and that any portion of it, however minute, is, as to color, complete in itself. [11]

EMBROIDERY FRAME.

Embroidery frame of the mid-19th century. Frames like this one could be adjusted for various sizes of embroidery, up to 1¼ yards wide, and were very suitable for making hearth rugs.

Undoubtedly, throughout the 19th century many rugs were embroidered in patterns that reflected current fashionable trends, such as the large cross-stitched carpet with a reclining dog as a central motif from the Strong Museum collection in Rochester, New York. Many others were embroidered in the decorative traditions of distant home-lands. One early-19th-century Pennsylvania rug, embroidered in cross-stitch, sets traditional stars, doves and floral motifs off against a light, olive-green background.

Throughout the century embroidery "rages" followed each other; one, in 1877, made use of salvaged yarns ravelled from tapestry carpet. These were called "carpet mats," and the variegated printed warp yarns provided the material. Embroidering these mats was such a popular pastime that carpet merchants were able to sell samples, scraps and ends of carpeting which normally were waste goods. [12]

Just as the bed rugs of the 18th century were carefully thought out, planned and made in quality new materials, so are the rugs which are embroidered in the third quarter of the 20th century. Small rugs as well as room-sized ones are being worked all over the United States in contemporary motifs as well as in adaptations of quilting, Chinese and near eastern rugs and embroidery designs. One canvas embroidery rug, worked in memory of a friend, includes birds and flowers indigenous to a Pocono Mountain region in Pennsylvania. Each woman worked a section of the pattern which had been planned out in advance and, when the embroidery was completed, the various sections were joined and finished. Materials are no longer grown and processed at home: they can now be purchased in countless shops at considerable cost—as plain canvas and yarn, pre-painted and designed canvas in stock, or custom patterns as pre-packaged kits which include needle, yarn and patterned canvas are also available.

Embroidered rugs can also be designed at home, adapted or made directly from patterns and instructions included in the myriad ladies' magazines—sometimes planned with color schemes to match a particular room. For durability, most are worked in various canvas stitches, although the needle-knotted adaptation of the shaggy pile, Scandinavian Rya rug might also fall within the embroidery category. Like the Pliney Moore, Caswell and some minor carpets of the 19th century, embroidered rugs today also require skill, time and often the services of professionals to finish, for instance, stitching together the sections, blocking and backing. They are still luxurious floor-coverings produced for personal pleasure and comfort and still a floor covering for the wealthy.

One of the 1859 patterns from the *Ladies' Hand Book of Fancy and Ornamental Work*, suitable for a worsted-work hearth rug, table or sofa cover.

11 Custom Carpets

Opposite:
Detail of a large, embroidered flame-patterned textile which, according to Historic Deerfield Inc., Deerfield, Massachusetts, is a carpet. This textile, which is very similar in technique, pattern and construction to examples at Winterthur and Williamsburg, may, however, have originally been used as a table or bed covering rather than a carpet.

Americans have, since early times, desired beautiful rugs, using them wherever and whenever they could. In 1788 a Frenchman, Brissot de Warville, commented: ". . . it is a favorite taste with the Americans; they receive it from the interested avarice of their old masters the English."[1] They used them on stairs, in halls, passages, parlors, and dining rooms. In the 1860s carpeting had been adopted as a semi-necessity, the great floral patterns used, as Kettell wrote in *Eighty Years Progress*, "in a thousand places where, in other parts of the world, it is never seen . . . He does not hesitate to spread every place where he is accustomed to tread with a due quantity of three-ply or tapestry or Brussels or Turkey."[2]

As carpeting became ever more accessible and inexpensive, with improved weaving technology, its use spread throughout the United States, in houses and public buildings, on riverboats and trains, in automobiles and airplanes. Gradually it spread over the floors in parlors, halls and bedrooms, and later into bathrooms, kitchens, porches and gardens. Running parallel with the desire for large carpeted areas there has traditionally been the desire for something uniquely personal. Early hooked, braided and yarn-sewn rugs were made in the home, for reasons of either economy or elegance; they each had a uniqueness which machine-made carpets could not offer. The prevailing desire for comfort combined with a uniquely personal quality led to the manufacture of

Spectacular late 1860s or early 1870s interior of the Bristol and Providence steamers on the route between Boston and New York. Similar elegant steamships, along with the railroads, appointed with fashionable carpeting and furnishings, introduced many Americans to the luxury of carpeting underfoot.

Overleaf:
A sunken "conversation pit" in which floor, sofa and cushions are covered in luxurious, shag-tufted carpet was a fashionable seating environment in America in the 1960s and early 70s.

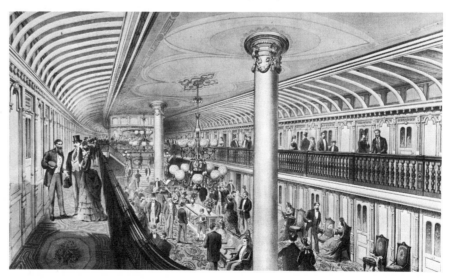

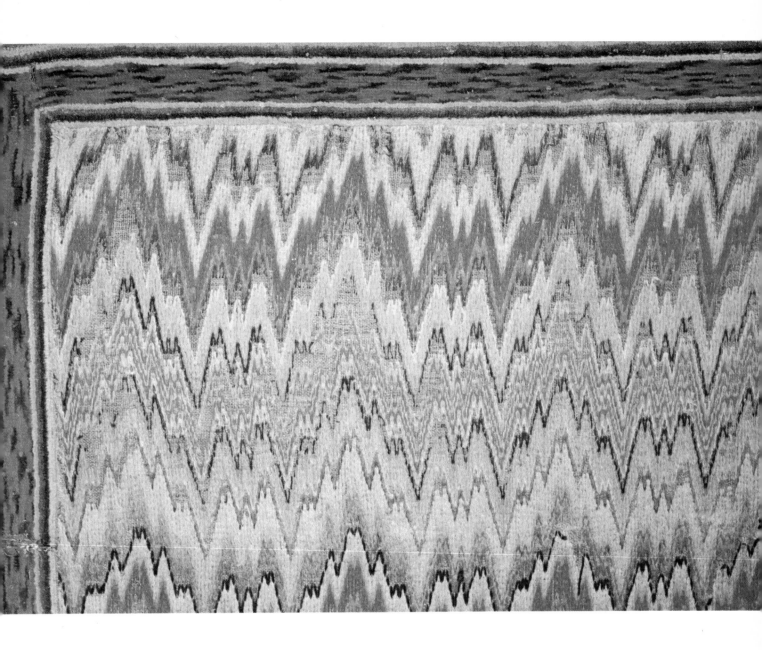

Left and below:
Sleeping coach and drawing
room coach of the Erie Railway
in 1876, with fashionable,
elegant wall-to-wall carpeting
and runners.

Wilton carpet designed and
made for Baltimore and Ohio
Railroad Pullman cars by the
Bigelow-Sanford Company
during the mid-1930s.

floor or "fifth wall" coverings which were designed sometimes by clients
themselves, often by designers or custom manufacturers, all to a personal
specification, thus providing a product to exacting specifications tufted and
finished by hand in custom workshops.

As long ago as 1860, when William Morris in England championed a return
to the forms and processes of medieval hand crafts, we can see the strength of
reaction to the manufactured vulgarity that had become a product of the industrial revolution. Morris became involved not only in unified design, but also
in handcrafting fabrics and rugs.[3] By 1879 these "arts and crafts" design
concepts had been adopted and expanded by Louis C. Tiffany, Samuel Cole-
man and Candace Wheeler, who organized one of the earliest design firms in
America, known as the Associated Artists. They dictated the fashion to their

Overleaf:
"Floorscape," a woven and
knotted, hand-crafted floor
environment in three sections
executed in 1972 by Yvonne
Bobrowicz.

Opposite:
"I've Grown Accustomed to her
Pace." This subtle, deeply
carved custom wall tapestry
designed by Edward Fields, Inc.
required hours of hand labor to
tuft and sculpt even though
electric tufting "guns" and
shearing clippers were used.

clients, in many cases designing decorative motifs and detailing for wallpaper, and textiles to produce a unified concept. When the partnership dissolved in 1883, Candace Wheeler retained the name and pursued an independent course, designing wallpapers and textiles and organizing women's groups to encourage home industries by reviving old craft forms.[4] Her two books, *Principles of Home Decoration* and *How to Make Rugs,* gave simple practical instructions on how to obtain unified design. Rugs with alternating light weft and dark warp or vice versa must be, she wrote, "studiously and carefully combined to produce the best results."[5]

By the early 20th century, others had joined the movement. Albert Herter, best known for his murals and tapestry series of New York, designed and executed several tapestry-weave rugs with Art Nouveau and later Art Deco patterns. Perhaps Frank Lloyd Wright, however, reflected to the greatest extent Morris's philosophy of unity. In his design studios he carried out the completion of his architectural concept through paying attention to the finest detailing—from the exterior of the building down to light switches, door knobs and carpeting. Some of the carpets were hand-knotted beige, imported from outside America, some custom-tufted for Wright in the 1940s by Edward Fields, Inc., which has since continued the association with the Frank Lloyd Wright Foundation.

Cranbrook Academy, founded in 1925, became an important American design center. There, under a master/apprentice system, skills of handcrafting and the principles of good design were taught which could be applied to the realities of modern technology, in "attempts to elevate the quality of manufactured goods by designing for industry."[6] Eliel and Loja Saarinen were

Hand-woven, knotted-pile rug in gray, brown, beige and gold camel hair. Designed by Eliel and Loja Saarinen in 1930 for the dining-room of their Cranbrook residence.

invited to the United States in the 1920s to design and direct the Academy. It was to be based on a concept of total, integrated design, which was executed in the school workshops. Loja, a weaver, was in charge of creating all the textiles used at the school and in the faculty residences. Many of these rugs which they designed are still, after fifty years, in houses at Cranbrook, in their museum and at the Kingswood School, a private boarding-school. Many fine weavers were trained, taught or wove there; they are part of a tradition which continues today.

It was during the period of the 1920s and 1930s with the new design concepts of Wright and Saarinen, the founding of Cranbrook, and demand for custom rugs—something special, something unique, something personal—that the circle of custom carpet-makers began to expand. The craze for Early American was in full swing by the 1920s. Because of widespread demand encouraged by several lucrative auctions of old hooked rugs at Sotheby, Parke Bernet in New York, many rugs, often enormous, were custom hooked in Early American scroll, floral, and patchwork adapted patterns. Percellen, Priscilla Turner, the Porters, V'Soske, Lillian Mills-Mosseller, George Wells are names associated with the early custom hooked rug business.

Percy and Ellen Porter, the English immigrants to Long Island who first made a hooked rug using a bath towel as a backing, began making hooked rugs in traditional patterns in all sizes to specifications of their customers—rugs designed for particular rooms. Known as Purcellen or Porter rugs, they were made entirely in a small studio called the "Ruggery" on Long Island. There the rugs were designed, the wools dyed, and the carpets hooked, bound and sheared by the Porters, neighborhood women, and students.

Daring geometric Art Deco pattern in shades of rust, black and cream, designed by M. Wirde at Cranbrook, *c.* 1930.

Left:
Rug hooked with hand-punch needle by George Wells translates garden bounty into a delectable floor covering.

Right:
Hooked rug by George Wells, 1970, incorporating family, houses, pets and sports is characteristic of the personal custom rug.

The shuttle hook was the original method of production at the V'Soske workshop. Now rugs are usually made with a special electric single-needle tufting gun which resembles an electric drill.

When George Wells took over the Ruggery in 1955, many of his rugs were experiments in geometric abstract patterns, combining a variety of available materials. However, like most of the custom rugmakers, he ultimately used only wool yarns for hooking in order to obtain closely controlled quality, color and texture in the finished product. In the mid-1950s he developed a type of custom hooked rug about 12 inches wide and several feet long, made by veterans under his own supervision, as part of a rehabilitation project. These rugs could be used as decorative accents in front of sofas, sideboards, or beds.

Gradually requests for personal designs incorporating family history, favorite hobbies, sports, pets or occasions were made, hooked in special designs and color schemes. One worked by George Wells, at the request of a customer, hooked the footprint of a beloved dog into a seashell-bordered rug. Lillian Mills-Mosseller of North Carolina worked with mountain artisans who had always hooked rugs in traditional patterns and colors. She learned to dye yarns to enable her to teach the artisans new patterns in new colors. She designed carpets for the first Ladies' Galleries in the Smithsonian Institution, which were adapted from an Abraham Lincoln letter, a period photograph of the Blue Room during the Grant administration, and interiors of the fashionable mid-19th-century riverboats. She, too, produced a wide variety of picture rugs, including one for the Little White House of Franklin D. Roosevelt in Warm Springs, Georgia.

Using principles of the traditional hooked rugs, the V'Soske family—to "try for an elegance that seemed to be missing from American carpets"— began in 1924 to make custom carpets in Grand Rapids, Michigan, a thriving furniture center.[7] With original designs, textures and color schemes, custom tufted rugs became and remain a specialty.

The V'Soske family also created rugs as an art form. Designs by prominent American artists including Stuart Davis, Margurite Zorach and Arschile

Gorky were translated by V'Soske into rugs. They were suitable for wall hangings as well as floor coverings. Some of them were exhibited in 1942 at the Museum of Modern Art.

Removed by time from the hooked rugs of the 1920s and 1930s, Edward Fields, with the same inventive spirit which characterized other rug entrepreneurs in America, began creating custom tufted broadloom in 1948 as a sideline to a wholesale carpet business. Wall-to-wall velvet carpet was "the look" which in 1948 was advertised as making rooms look bigger and easier to maintain. In order to be competitive with his smaller output, in 1953 he introduced "area rugs."[8] These were rugs designed and sized to define a limited living area. Area rugs were created to explode the myth that wall-to-wall carpeting made the room look bigger. They could be turned or moved within a room, patterned to disguise soil, and were easily transportable. The floor gradually became the fifth wall, to be treated as a painting perhaps, or as an extension of the wall. Recently super graphics have been converted into rugs for floors and for walls—the beginning of a new trend for wall tapestries, perhaps.

Some of these custom rugs and carpets adapt color or design concepts to a particular need. Others are "one of a kind," produced either in the custom rug

One of the carpets entitled "Flying Carpet" designed for the 1942 exhibition at the Museum of Modern Art by Stuart Davis, woven by V'Soske. Size: 7 feet 1 inch by 10 feet.

Floor environment created by Urban Jupena about 1975 which envelops seating elements in deep pile, hand-woven carpet.

workshops or exclusively by individual craftsmen, as experimental pieces or as custom-tailored commissions. Some fall within the framework of traditional floor coverings, regular shapes, woven or knotted by hand. Others fall within experimental categories of "environments" such as those designed by Urban Jupena or Yvonne Bobrowicz. These environments translate natural rock or earth forms into sculptured shapes sometimes encompassing not only the floor, but the walls and ceiling as well.[9] Some are modular, with repeating or individual sections, which can be combined and rearranged.

Custom hand-wrought rugs, long ago the substitute for the unobtainable, have today found a personal expression in the revival of the old forms and in the practice of old handcraft skills. Handcrafted, hooked, embroidered, knotted and latchhook rugs are now available in craft centers throughout the United States. Rug making is a craft no longer dominated by men as early carpet making was, nor any longer solely the creative work of women. With more leisure time in America, there is time to make a rug, a useful object, and one to which its maker can point with pride and say, "I made it."

Many of the new floor coverings are area rugs, used to define a living area, large or small, providing color contrasts against a neutral background of wood, practical, neutral wall-to-wall carpeting or one of the new easy care vinyl floor coverings. Sometimes old, sometimes new, sometimes custom made or handcrafted, sometimes a well-machined rendition, the area rug brings together the elegance of rugs that were in the beginning the privilege of the wealthy, with the simple handcrafted forms—matting, floor cloths and rag rugs that were inexpensive substitutes for the many people for whom the promise of America was that someday, they too, could have a fine rug in the parlor.

Notes

Alternate Floors

1 Kocher, p. 24.
2 Ibid., p. 21.
3 Ibid., p. 25.
4 Dow, pp. 17–18, "Everyday Life in the Massachusetts Bay Colony."
5 *American Domestic Cyclopaedia*, p. 516.
  The *American Domestic Cyclopaedia* included a recipe for cleaning wooden floors as follows:

  The dirtiest of floors may be rendered beautifully clean by the following process: First scrub with sand, then rub with a lye of caustic soda, using a stiff brush, and rinse off with warm water. Just before the floor is dry, moisten with dilute hydrochloric acid and then with a thin paste of bleaching powder (hypochlorite of lime). Let this remain over night, and wash in the morning.

6 As reported in Little, *Floor Coverings in New England before 1850*, p. 4.
7 Dilliard, p. 86.
8 Roth, p. 48.
9 Ibid., p. 48.
10 Kocher, p. 9.
11 Museum of Early Southern Decorative Arts Newspaper File, *South Carolina Gazette*; and *Country Journal*, Charleston, 4 March 1766, 1–2.

BENJAMIN HAWES SELLS ALL SORTS OF OIL and *Colours*, dry and prepared by Wholesale and Retail, viz. White and red lead, Venetian red, Stone, spruce, cake & English Ochre, Purple and Spanish broan, Umber, English, French and distilled verdigrise, Flake white, India red, Callums earth, Tarrawert, Gold size and litharge, Kings and Naples yellow, Bister, Blue vice, Lump and powder lampblack, Black lead, Roll brimstone, Powderedd [*sic*] Dutch brass, Gold and Silver leaf, Glue, size and whiting, Hard and common varnish, Red and white argil, Nut galls, French Berries, Chip and ground logwood; Linseed, drying. turpentine, nut, grape, palm, olive; Genoa, Florence, train, white, chamberlamb, neat foot and fish oils; Blue and green vediter; English, Dutch & Brown pink; Carmine, Vermilion, Drop Lake, Prussian Blue, Yellow and red Orpiment, Sap green, Gumbouge, White copperas, Shells of all colours, Brushes and tools of all sorts, Pencils of all kinds, Pallat boards and knives, Paint stones and mullers, Red chalk, India ink, Blue black, Turpentine varnish and oil of tar, Rotten stone, Pitch and tar, Bees wax, Hogs Eard, Black and yellow rosin, Common turpentine;

Gum fandarack, arabeck, seneca and dragon; Fine calcind and stowing finals [*sic*],
Fig and flat indico [*sic*], Blacking balls, Fullers earth, scouring paper, Neat glass
lanthorns; Crown, Bristol, Newcastle and sheet glass, cut to any dimension;
Glaziers diamonds, &c. &c.; Florey black, Ivory black.

12 Litchfield Historical Society, Litchfield, Connecticut.

13 Excellent reference paintings at New York Historical Association, Cooperstown, New York and Abby Aldrich Rockefeller Folk Art Collection,
Williamsburg, Virginia.

14 Little, *American Decorative Wall Painting, 1700–1850*, pp. 76–7. From
Rufus Porter, *A Select Collection of Valuable and Curious Arts and Interesting
Experiments.*

To Paint In Figures For Carpets Or Borders—Take a sheet of pasteboard or
strong paper, and paint thereon with a pencil any flower or figure that would be
elegant for a border or carpet figure; then with small gouges and chissels, or a
sharp penknife, cut out the figure completely, that it may be represented by
apertures cut through the paper. Lay this pattern on the ground intended to
receive the figure, whether a floor or painted cloth, and with a smooth brush
paint with a quick vibrative motion over the whole figure. Then take the paper
and you will have an entire figure on the ground.

15 Fraser, pp. 296–300.

16, 17 Ibid., p. 300, 296.

Matting

1 Dow, pp. 5–6, 17–18.
2 Ibid., p. 16.
3 Kocher, p. 10.
4 Little, *American Art Journal*, p. 112.
5 Kocher, p. 10.
6 Roth, p. 26.
7 Ibid., p. 30.
8 Hale, Edward Everett, *A New England Boyhood*, Boston, 1893, p. 1, 4–6.
9 Beecher, *American Woman's Home*, pp. 85–7.
10 Andrews, *The Community Industries of the Shakers*, pp. 186–7.
11 *What Every One Should Know*, pp. 286–7.
12 *The Carpet Trade*, Jan. 1877, p. 17.
13 *The Carpet Trade*, June 1877, p. 17.
14 Ibid.
15 Sears, Roebuck & Company No. 111 (1902).
16 By One Who Knows, p. 21.
17 Burt, p. 235.

From Rags to Riches

1 Roth, p. 46.
2 Lanier, pp. 33–4.

3 Ibid., p. 35. Collection of Colonial Williamsburg.

4 Roth, p. 46.

5 *Antiques,* "Clues and Footnotes," March 1971. From Leonard Withington *The Puritan: A Series of Essays,* 1836, Vol. 1, pp. 13–15.

6 Little, *Floor Coverings in New England before 1850,* p. 28.

7 Wheeler, pp. 58, 59, 100.

8 N. A., *Household Conveniences,* p. 181.

9 Archival materials of E. C. Beetem & Son, courtesy of the William Penn Historical Museum, Harrisburg, Pa.

10 Ibid.

11 Little, *Floor Coverings in New England before 1850,* p. 32.

12 Feeley.

13 Wheeler, p. 129.

14 The entire set of instructions for "shaggy mats" from *What Every One Should Know* follows:

Get a pair of very coarse steel knitting needles and some jute twine—no other will answer—the same that is used in making gunny-sacks, and can always be obtained where they are made, if not at the shops. Set up fifteen stitches on the needles, and knit once across; knit the first stitch on the second row, and between the needles put a piece of the cloth at right angles with the stitch, and knit another stitch; then turn the end of the cloth that points toward you out between the needles, so that the ends will be even, and so on clear across, two stitches to every piece of cloth; then knit across again plain to get back to the side where you began. The ends of the cloth must always point from you as you knit them in. . . . it is a good way to use up discarded coats, vests and pants. The cloth must not be too thick; broadcloth, waterproof, ladies' cloth, etc., are the best for the purpose. Mine is really very pretty; the center is orange and black mixed waterproof and a border of black, brightened up with tufts of scarlet flannel.

15 For extensive discussion and illustration of sewn rugs and hooked rugs, see Kopp, *American Hooked and Sewn Rugs.*

16 Fraser, p. 229.

17 Frost Descriptive Catalogue, p. 4.

18 Ibid.

19 Ross Pattern Book, n.d.

20 Kopp, *American Hooked and Sewn Rugs,* pp. 87–8.

21 Ibid.

22 Ibid., p. 87.

23 Klamkin, p. 100.

24 Andrews, *Shaker Furniture,* p. 55.

25 Ibid., p. 54.

26 Andrews, *Community Industries of the Shakers,* pp. 186–7.

27 Klamkin, p. 16.

Floorcloths, Oilcloths and Linoleums

1 Roth, p. 10.

2 Kocher, p. 12.

3 Little, *American Decorative Wall Painting*, p. 76.

4 Little, *Floor Coverings in New England before 1850*, pp. 21–2.

5 *Antiques*, April 1971, p. 588.

6 *The Carpet Trade*, Aug. 1876.

7 Webster, T. and Parkes, p. 256.

8 Roth, p. 28.

9 Wainwright, p. 43.

10 Roth, p. 28.

11 *Household Conveniences*, pp. 181–2.

12 Hummel, "Floorcoverings," Irene Emery Roundtable Proceedings 1975, pp. 73–4.

13 Little, *American Decorative Wall Painting*, p. 77.

14 Little, *Floor Coverings in New England before 1850*, pp. 18–21; Roth, pp. 13, 25.

15 Kocher, p. 7.

16 Roth, pp. 13–14; Little, *Floor Coverings in New England before 1850*, pp. 20–1.

17 Lanier, p. 32; Roth, p. 16.

18 Lanier, ibid.; Roth, ibid.

19 Sherrill, p. 150.

20 Cole, *Encyclopedia of Dry Goods*, pp. 293–4; *The Carpet Trade*, October 1875.

21 Webster, T. and Parkes, pp. 508, 890.

22 "Grandma used to give me my bath every Saturday night in a large brass kettle behind the pot-bellied stove which stood on a large square of linoleum called 'oilcloth' in those days." A recollection by Mrs. Rae McGrady Booth, related in "Memoirs of an Iowa Farm Girl," *Annals of Iowa*, Fall 1966.

23 The Armstrong Cork Company archival materials.

Flatwoven Carpets

1 *Maryland Gazette*, Annapolis, 25 June 1752, 2–3, Museum of Early Southern Decorative Arts newspaper file.

2 Ibid., 24 July 1760.

3 Little, *American Art Journal*, p. 111.

4 Kimball, p. 378.

5 *Virginia Gazette or Norfolk Intelligencer*, 14 July 1774, 4–1, Museum of Early Southern Decorative Arts newspaper file. 10 quarters = 2½ yds.

6 Roth, p. 33.

7 Cole and Williamson, p. 29.

8 Ibid., p. 26.

9 Ibid., pp. 30–57.

10 A. and E. S. Higgins catalogue, n.d.

11 Cole and Williamson, p. 15.

12 Chapman, p. 31.

13 Cole and Williamson, p. 8.

14 Chapman, p. 22.

15 Cole and Williamson, p. 101.

16 Sears, Roebuck Catalogue, 1902, p. 901.

17 Wheeler, p. 57.

18 Ibid., pp. 57–63.

19 Ibid., p. 61.

20 Cole, p. 87.

21 Ibid.

22 Cole, *Encyclopedia of Dry Goods*, p. 87.

23 Roth, p. 47.

24 Cole and Williamson, pp. 28, 31, 32.

25 Boyd, *Popular Arts of Spanish New Mexico*, p. 182.

26 Ibid., p. 185.

27 Cox, p. 26.

28 Ibid.

29 Boyd, p. 187. From *Down the Santa Fe Trail and Into Mexico 1846–7*, Susan Shelby Magoffin, Yale University Press, 1926.
Note : Examples of jerga can be found in the collections of the Millicent Rogers Museum, Taos, New Mexico, and The Museum of International Folk Art, Santa Fe, New Mexico.

30 Kahlenberg, p. 6.

31 Amsden, p. 133.

32 Kahlenberg, p. 15.

33 Amsden, p. 193.

34 Dedera, Chapter 6.

35 Dedera, p. 44. Term coined by Gilbert Maxwell, an Indian trader, in 1963.

Brussels, Wilton and Tapestry

1 Little, *Floor Coverings in New England before 1850*, p. 12.

2 Cole and Williamson, p. 32.

3 Tattersall, pp. 120–2.

4 Both samples are in the collection of the Museums at Stony Brook.

5 Roth, p. 35.

6 Ibid., p. 36.

7 Little, *American Art Journal*, p. 111.

8 Prime, 1929, p. 209.

9 Ewing, p. 16.

10 Bigelow, p. 37.

11 Cole and Williamson, p. 69.

12 Collection of The Brooklyn Museum.

13 Eastlake, pp. 47–8.

14 Eastlake, pp. 112–13.

15 Beecher and Stowe, pp. 85–7.

16 N.A., *Household Conveniences*, p. 181.

17 Cook, *House Beautiful*, p. 55.

Turkey Work, Axminster and Chenille

1 Sherrill, p. 142. For extensive documentation on the use of oriental carpets in America, see this article.

2 Lanier, pp. 6–11.

3 Lanier, p. 3.

4 Ibid., p. 59.

5 Dow, *Arts and Crafts in New England,* p. 114.

6 Roth, p. 6.

7 Sherrill, p. 150.

8 Cook, *What Shall We Do With Our Walls?,* p. 14.

9 Chapman, p. 24.

10 Detweiler.

11 Tattersall, p. 67.

12 In 1779, a visitor to the factory of Whitty recorded that there was a "row of children properly so called, for none of them I think could exceed twelve to fourteen, sitting close to each other, the whole breadth of the carpet with every stitch of the pattern before them, which they executed with surprising dexterity and dispatch." Tattersall, p. 69.

13 Ibid., p. 62.

14 This carpet was likewise described in the Pennsylvania *Journal* of 8 June 1791.

15 Cole and Williamson, p. 33.

16 Cole, p. 83.

17 Montgomery Ward Catalogue, 1895.

18 Cole and Williamson, p. 116.

19 *Carpet Trade,* Vol. 7, 1876, p. 17.

20 Cole and Williamson, p. 102.

21 Montgomery Ward Catalogue, 1895.

22 de Wolfe, p. 201.

Tufted Carpets

1 The tufted carpet industry, using revolutionary new technology to produce an age-old product, ranks among the American growth industries which include television, computers, petroleum-based fiber products. It was only with the widespread use of tufting, beginning in the 1950s, that yardage production radically increased.
1899—76 million square yards of carpet per year.
1952—81 million square yards of carpet per year.
1960—148 million square yards of carpet per year.
1975—703 million square yards of carpet per year.

2 In 1950 carpeting with a wool pile was available from $6.26 per square yard. In 1977, tufted carpeting using exclusively synthetic yarns and backing is available at prices ranging upwards from $3.90 per yard.

3 Once the floorcovering used only in residences, carpeting has gradually spread to other floors—cars, subways, airplanes, and only since the 1960s has there been widespread use of commercial carpeting—in hospitals, schools, libraries, offices and restaurants.

4 The tufting machine alone could not have revolutionized the industry in terms of production because natural raw materials, especially wool, in the quantities required to produce over 700 million yards of carpeting are not

available. The development of Nylon and other monofilament fibers during World Warr II—which are less expensive and available in seemingly unending supplies—has permitted this enormous expansion.

Embroidered Carpets

1 Lanier, p. 13.
2 *Times*, Charleston, 21 January 1802, 3–4, Museum of Early Southern Decorative Arts newspaper file.
3 English embroidered carpets are in several American museums, including Winterthur, The Metropolitan Museum, Colonial Williamsburg and The Brooklyn Museum.
4 *Bed Ruggs 1722–1833* lists towns where the patterned bed rugs were found, and the names of owners or makers when known. It is possible that a less elaborate form of bed rug was made in other parts of the Eastern United States.
5 Kopp, *American Hooked and Sewn Rugs*, p. 14.
6 Ibid., p. 21.
7 Later 19th-century hooked "fancy rugs" with a raised and sculptured pile were known as Waldoboro rugs, from Waldoboro, Maine, the area in which they were most frequently made. They are extensively discussed in *American Hooked and Sewn Rugs*.
8 Faraday, p. 280.
9 Ibid.
10 Records at Shelburne Museum, *Antiques*, June 1926.
11 Hartley, pp. 236–7.
12 *The Carpet Trade*, 1877.

Custom Carpets

1 Landreau, p. 4.
2 Cole and Williamson, p. 82.
3 One of the Morris rugs is believed to be in the Newport, Rhode Island summer cottage, "The Breakers."
4 Faude, pp. 100, 101, 127, 128.
5 Wheeler, p. 51.
6 *The Creative Spirit of Cranbrook: The Early Years*, p. 4. Louise (Loja) was also influential in introducing the concept that weaving was not solely a utilitarian craft but an art as well.
7 *National Geographic*, pp. 122–6, 776–8.
8 The term "Area Rug" was coined by Edward Fields, a carpet manufacturer and Raymond Loewy, an important industrial designer in America at that time.
9 One environment of Urban Jupena's, encompassing floor, wall and ceiling, is illustrated in the Smithsonian Institution's catalogue "America Underfoot."

Ingrain Pattern Chronology

These photographs trace stylistic changes in ingrain carpeting patterns from the late 18th century until the end of widespread manufacture in the early 20th century. Late-18th- and early-19th-century patterns are small, regular geometrics with motifs set off against unpatterned backgrounds. By the 1830s a larger scale prevails, with the emphasis on diagonal arrangement, and there is the introduction of curvilinear and leaf forms in clear reds, maroons, golds, olive greens and cream. By the 1860s the patterns are more circular, with wreath and sunburst motifs, an even larger scale, and increased background detailing in a color palette dominated by greens, red, maroon, browns and white. In the third quarter of the 19th century, large-scale patterns incorporate near-eastern motifs and elaborate scrolled leaves in disrupted patterns; colors include tobacco, mushroom and gold, sometimes set off against harsh aniline dyes. The period 1875-1900 is dominated by diaper patterns, oriental adaptations, rococo and gothic revival motifs, but eventually the drab or harsh aniline colors and repetitive patterns of the late 19th and early 20th centuries, as well as the use of inferior materials, herald the end of the popular ingrains.

Late 18th century

Late 18th century

Late 18th or early 19th century

1800–35

1825–50

1830–50

1838

Late 18th century or up to 1822

1830–60

1840–60   front

1840–60   reverse

1840–60

1850–75

1850–75

1850–60

c.1860

1860–80

c.1860

1853–60

1850–60

1860–80

1860–80

1860–75

1860–70

1870

c.1870

1850–75

c.1870

c.1870

1870–80

1870–1900

1870–1900

1870–1900   1870–1900   1874   c.1870

1875–1900   1884   1880–1900   1880–1900

1880–1900   1884   1880–1900   1896

1880–1900   1900–10   1900–10   1900–19

Brussels, Wilton and Tapestry Pattern Chronology

Brussels, Wilton and tapestry are combined here because of the similarity of their construction (see pages 112–23). Unfortunately, few 18th-century carpet examples survive as testimony to the patterns of the period. Fragments and complete carpets of the first half of the 19th century, however, show that geometric patterns and ones based on strapwork or floral diagonals were commonly available. By mid-century, although there is some near-eastern influence, large-scale florals and scrolls in naturalistic shadings dominated by maroon, red and olive, with accents of brown, cream and blue, are the most prevalent. By the 1870s the leaf and scroll patterns are interrupted and the overall look, in tobacco, off-grays and browns, is much more cluttered. Diaper and Persian patterns begin to appear and, by the turn of the century, large naturalistic flowers, Persian and Turkish motifs and elaborate border detailing on rugs are fashionable again. The Chinese mode takes over during the 1920s, to be superseded by the monochrome broadloom velvets in, among other tones, beige, tan and taupe. During the 1940s and '50s sculptured pile and velvets in muted pastels gradually give way to the new tufted carpets in tweedy shags. Today, contemporary woven cut-and-looped pile Wilton is available in many colors and patterns and considered a luxury carpet.

Brussels, 1820–30 (English)

Brussels, 1840–50 (English)

Brussels, 1840–50 (English)

Brussels, c.1850 (English)

Brussels, 1851 (English)

Wilton, c.1845

Wilton, c.1845–50

Tapestry, c.1845–50

Tapestry, c.1851

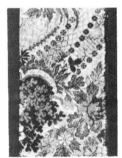
Brussels, c.1875

Wilton, 1881

Wilton, 1875–1900

Top: Brussels, *bottom:* Wilton; c.1900–10

Wilton, c.1920–30

Wilton, 1900–30

Wilton, c.1930

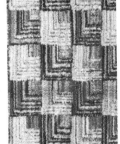
Brussels, 1932

Brussels, 1935–50

Wilton, 1976

Glossary

AREA RUG: decorative rug which defines a living space in a room by providing a colorful focus on a monotone surface of carpet, parquet, stone or tile. Used either singly or in combination with others. A term coined in the 1950s.

ART SQUARES or BIG FLOOR RUGS: an ingrain carpet innovation of about 1895 woven in one piece with borders and fringe at both ends. Available in wool, cotton, jute or combinations. Could be used as crumbcloths, druggets or rugs to cover worn carpet. Popular because they didn't have to fit a room exactly, were less cumbersome than wall to wall, easy to remove and clean and were inexpensive.

AUBUSSON CARPETS: flat- and pile-woven carpets made in Aubusson in the south of France from c. 1665 onwards. The tapestry woven carpets, popular in the 18th and especially the late 19th centuries, characterized by soft colors in rococo, floral and scroll patterns and usually backed with a cloth lining. The thick pile carpets woven in imitation of the Savonnerie weaving techniques.

AXMINSTER: originally a hand-knotted, 18th century English carpet imitating Turkish carpets. Machine-woven Axminsters, perfected in the 1870s, closely resemble the hand-knotted originals.

BACKING: woven or non-woven foundation material usually burlap or synthetic which also controls dimensional stability in linoleums, resilient floorings and certain carpets.

BACKING CLOTH: cotton or jute fabrics of varying weight used as the backing in the manufacture of linoleum and oil cloth.

BARREL LOOM or CYLINDER LOOM: a loom with a pattern-control mechanism resembling a music box, said to be patented by Thomas Morton of Kilmarnock, Scotland, in 1800.

BATTEN, COMB or LAY: the swinging bar, part of the loom used to beat or force the weft yarns into the web of a woven fabric.

BATTLESHIP LINOLEUM: high quality standard set by the U.S. Bureau of Standards for linoleum used for government purposes.

B.C.F.: bulked continuous filament nylon, particularly suitable to looped-pile constructions because the fibers are trilubular or triskelion instead of round and therefore have excellent surface-covering properties.

BEAM: large horizontal spool at the end of a loom. The warp threads are wound on to one with flanges at the start; the finished carpet on a take-up roller at the end of the weaving process.

BEARDING: long fibered fuzz on loop-pile fabrics caused by inadequate anchorage into the backing, and by snagging.

BEAT UP or BEATING UP: a process in weaving in which new weft is forced into the fabric. The term for the number of tufts per lengthwise inch of pile in non-wire carpet construction such as Axminster and chenille. Equivalent to the term "wire" in the construction of Brussels and Wilton.

BEATING UP: the point in the weaving process at which the weft shots or pile are forced into the body of the fabric after the shuttle crosses the shed.

BENT NEEDLES: tufting-machine needles which are permanently out of alignment and cause a streak running lengthwise in the carpet from the uneven spacing. In a Jacquard attachment, a bent needle is one out of alignment with the punched hole in the pattern cards.

BINDING YARN: cotton or rayon yarn which runs lengthwise in a woven fabric to bind the pile tufts firmly. Sometimes called the crimp warp or binder warp.

BOBBIN: a spool of yarn carried either in a shuttle to provide the weft in a carpet or in the frames of a Brussel or Wilton loom to supply the colored warps.

BODY BRUSSELS: a term used to describe a heavy, resilient, multi-frame Brussels carpet, in which all the colored worsted pattern yarns are carried along with the body or structure of the carpet and picked up into the pattern as the design requires.

BODY: industry term originally referring to lengths of 27-inch-wide carpeting seamed together and bound to form a rug or wall-to-wall carpet, or to the seamed center of a bordered rug. Now used to describe the weight and fall of a carpet; also hand.

BONDED RUBBER CUSHIONING: a cushion of latex foam or sponge rubber bonded either to a carpet in the manufacturing process in strips or as a single width.

BORDER: width of edging of coordinated pattern, mitered at the corners and stitched to the body of either a rug or fitted wall-to-wall carpet. In vogue through the first quarter of the 20th century.

BRAIDED RUG: early American form made of uniform

strips of cloth, often of used material, folded in at the edges and either braided into lengths and stitched invisibly together with carpet threads or worked into the preceding row as the braiding progresses, eliminating the need for stitching.

BROADLOOM: a carpet woven in 54 inch or greater widths widely produced at the turn of the 20th century. The term is only an indication of width and has nothing to do with construction or quality. Eventually new 12 feet widths, now standard, eliminated unsightly seams and therefore encouraged the widespread use of monochrome carpet that began in the 1920s and 30s.

BROCADE: a carpet or rug, often a single color, in which a raised pattern or engraved effect is created by using heavy twisted-yarn tufts on a ground of straight fiber.

BROCHE CARPET: wool carpet with a patterned surface, formed by a clipped pile figure on a loop pile background.

BROOM CORN: a tall plant of the sorghum family brought from England in the late 18th century and successfully cultivated by the Shakers for making brooms. The top stem and seed tassel were dried, divided into lengthwise sections, stripped of seeds and the straws bound into a broom.

BRUSSELS CARPET also BODY BRUSSELS: a looped-pile carpet with a linen warp and weft and worsted pile. The pile formed over a wire was invented in Brussels about 1710. All the colors which appear in a single row of warp are carried along within the structure of the carpet controlled by a Jacquard. A frame or tray attached to the back of the loom holds spools of yarns—one frame required for each color in the pattern.

BRUSSELS STOUTS: inferior quality of Brussels carpet of the first quarter of the 20th century. The pile was less dense and part jute instead of all worsted.

BUCKLING also PUCKERS: bumps and ridges in a carpet surface preventing it from lying flat; caused by improper installation, uneven weaving, dimensional instability or mismatched carpet.

BURLAP: coarse plain-woven fabric usually of jute or hemp often used as a floor covering backing.

BURLING: carpet finishing operation in which missing tufts are replaced by hand.

BUTTON RUGS: hand-made pile rug composed of small fabric circles which have been folded in quarters, then stitched at the point on to a backing.

CARPET/CARPITT: a soft floor covering installed wall to wall and fastened down; also formerly used for wall-to-wall linoleum. Oriental carpets made in finished sizes are interchangeably known as rugs.

CARPET BALLS: narrow strips of rags, stitched together and wound into balls for use in making rag rugs.

CARPET BEATER: a wicker, rattan or wire paddle formerly used to beat the dust out of carpets hanging on a clothes line.

CARPET BEETLE or CARPET BUG: destructive reddish-brown European insect (Phylum Arthropoda) that came into the United States in the 1870s and whose larvae feast on woolen carpets and other animal fiber materials.

CARPET BINDING: a woven tape of wool or cotton used to bind the raw edges of carpets to prevent raveling.

CARPET MAT: mat embroidered with yarns raveled from tapestry carpets; popular about 1877.

CARPET PADDING: layer of material placed under the carpet to provide extra resiliency, prolong wear, deaden sound and insulate.

CARPET TACK: a sharp large headed tack about $\frac{1}{2}$ inch long of blued steel or copper used to hold wall-to-wall carpeting in place; also a two-pronged "U" shaped variety, especially suitable for fastening matting.

CARPET WOOL: low-grade, rough, straight wool, from unimproved breeds of sheep used in the manufacture of carpets; mostly imported from England, Asia Minor, India and South America.

CATERPILLAR RUG: early 19th-century shirred rug with pile formed by folded strips of variously colored fabric that are gathered into "caterpillars," then stitched on to a backing.

CEDAR BARK MATS: woodlands Indian matting woven from the inner bark of red cedar trees used as floor, door and bed coverings.

CHAIN: alternate term for the warp of a pile carpet that combines with the weft to form the woven structure required to hold the pile in place. See CRIMP.

CHENILLE also CHENILLE AXMINSTER: luxurious cut-pile carpet named after the French "caterpillar," produced on two looms—one to weave the chenille or fur, the other to weave the chenille into the carpet structure. The process is suitable for large sizes and custom shapes.

CONSTRUCTION: the factors that go into the weaving of a specific type of carpet, such as wires, stuffers, loom type, pitch, yarns, wire height, shots, frames, yarn count, total carpet weight, or their various equivalents.

CONTINUOUS FILAMENT YARN: synthetic fibers manufactured by an extension process which produces filaments of enormous length; used to make carpet yarns which are strong, require no spinning, and resist shedding.

COTTON COUNT: measure used to determine the cotton warp weight in a carpet based on the number of lengths of yarn, 840 yards long, to one pound.

CRIMP or TAKE-UP: curvature in the chain warp produced in the process of binding the structural elements into a finished woven carpet.

CROCHET RUG: washable hand-crafted rug made from strips of rags or yarn crocheted in any of several crochet stitches.

CROSS SEAMS, HEADINGS or TAB ENDS: half-inch strips of prints and cretonnes one yard long which are stitched together end to end, with alternating light and dark colors, to form a hit-and-miss effect in rag carpet weaving.

CRUMBCLOTH: cloth, often damask, formerly laid under a table to catch crumbs and protect the carpet. *See also* DRUGGET, SERGE.

CUSHIONING: vinyl foam core between the wear layer and backing which provides greater warmth and springiness in some of the resilient floorings of the 1970s.

CUT PILE: tufted or woven carpet with pile cut to an even length.

DENIER: a unit of weight used to express the size of a single continuous filament yarn of silk, rayon, nylon and other synthetic fibers. Equivalent to the number of grams per 9000 meters of a given yarn.

DENSITY: measure of the compactness of face or surface yarns in a carpet. Higher density usually indicates greater wearability.

DIMENSIONAL STABILITY: ability of a fabric, and especially a carpet, to maintain its original dimensions after use and wet cleaning.

DOLLAR MAT or RUG: floor covering in which decreasing sized circles of fabric have been appliquéd on to each other then on to the backing with overcast or button-hole stitches.

DOOR MAT: a small mat usually of jute, hemp, wire, woven rags or, today, AstroTurf, placed in front or inside of a door to catch dirt. One 19th-century interior variety known as "drawing-room door rugs."

DRAW LOOM: a complex hand-loom used to weave figured fabrics including ingrain and Brussels carpeting before the invention of the Jacquard.

DRAWN-IN RUGS: colloquial American term for hooked rugs used about 1900.

DROP MATCH: lengthwise pattern adjustment in seamed carpet required to maintain the overall design.

DRUGGET also called INDIA DRUGGET: coarse woolen or wool and linen fabric in solid colors, woven stripes or checks having less nap than baize. Used as an inexpensive 18th- and 19th-century substitute for carpets or as floorcloths.

ELL: old Flemish and Belgian measure of length equalling 27 inches which became the standard width for carpeting until the invention of the broadloom. *See also* QUARTER.

EMBOSSED CARPET: a carpet which has a high and low pile created by two types of yarn, one of which shrinks during the heat finishing process.

EMBOSSING: mechanical or chemical process used to create surface textures by depressing some elements of the pattern so that others stand out in relief.

EMBROIDERED RUGS: rugs or carpets with a surface embellished by canvas or crewel embroidery stitches.

FACE WEIGHT: a quality measure based on the number of ounces of surface yarn per square yard of carpet excluding the stuffers, backing yarns or secondary backing.

FELT BASE: asphalt-saturated felt developed in the early 20th century as a base for printed enamel floor coverings.

FELT RUG: inexpensive rug of felted wool or cattle hair sometimes with a printed or stenciled pattern used as carpeting or as padding under good carpets.

FIBER RUGS: reversible rugs of special paper yarns sometimes in combination with wool or cotton in twill or plain weave. Popular 20th-century summer carpet.

FLOCKING: a process for applying a carpet pile by permanently embedding electrostatically charged fibers into an adhesive surface.

FLOORCLOTH: generic term for a woven floor covering of wool or linen sometimes treated with oil paint. Used as or instead of carpet and also to protect or cover it.

FLUFF MATS or **SHAGGY MATS**: heavy knitted mats with a shaggy pile of short strips of fabric that are inserted as the knitting progresses. Used as hearth rugs or interior door mats.

FRIEZE or **TWIST**: hard twisted carpet yarn that creates a rough nubby texture.

FUSION BONDING: a manufacturing process in which pile is imbedded into a soft vinyl layer which hardens after curing. A second backing is then laminated to the vinyl to provide additional weight.

GAUGE or **GAGE**: a measurement of quality. In tufted or knitted carpet, the number of needles per crosswise inch; in resilient floor coverings, the thickness of the wearlayer. *See also* PITCH.

GRANITE CARPET: inexpensive, heavy-weight Sea Island cotton carpet resembling ingrain.

HARNESS: one of at least two horizontal bars which with the heddles are used to control the warp.

HEDDLES: a series of vertical cords or wires with an eye in the middle through which the warps are threaded.

HEMP CARPET: a woven carpet in which both warp and weft are made of plied hemp yarn.

HESSIAN PAPER: name for a special paper produced by processing pulp with zinc chloride, then subjecting it to pressure. *See also* PAPER CARPET.

INDOOR-OUTDOOR CARPET: solid-color or printed needle-punch carpet constructed entirely of synthetic fibers which makes it moisture- and wear-resistant. Suitable for use outdoors, in bathrooms and kitchens.

INGRAIN: American term for Scotch or Kidderminster, the flatwoven all-wool reversible carpet in which the design on the face is reproduced in reverse colors on the back. *See* PLY.

INLAID LINOLEUM: patterned linoleum in which all colors go through to the backing.

IRISH or **ERIN TAPESTRY**: an 1890s twill woven hemp carpet with printed pattern in exact imitation of Brussels.

JACQUARD: a loom attachment consisting of wires and perforated cards perfected by J. M. Jacquard in 1804, which automated and simplified the complicated pattern mechanism of the old draw loom; adapted to carpet manufacture in Philadelphia in the late 1820s.

JASPE: linoleum pattern in random striations in tones of a single color that create an appearance of texture (first half 20th century).

JUTE: a fiber from the sisal plant imported primarily from India and the Philippines; used for making stuffers, filling and backing for carpets.

KIDDERMINSTER: flatwoven reversible carpets named for the English weaving center where they were made; later known in 19th century America as ingrain.

KILMARNOCK. *See* SCOTCH.

KNITTED CARPET: originally a hand-crafted form of plain or patterned strips or blocks stitched together; now also a machine-knitted looped-pile carpet constructed on three sets of needles.

KRAFTCORD: tightly twisted yarns of processed wood pulp sometimes used as substitute for cotton and jute in carpet manufacture to provide stiffness and a smooth, clean back.

LEVEL LOOP: pile carpet of any construction in which all the loops are of equal height and form the surface.

LINOLEUM: originally a plain colored durable floor covering made of linseed oil, cork, wood, flour and paint pigments pressed into a burlap or canvas backing; invented in England in 1864, manufactured and widely used in the U.S. until 1974; remains the popular generic term for similar floor coverings of contemporary materials.

LIST: selvage or other narrow strips of fabric used as the weft in early American carpets, often referred to as list carpets.

MATCH MARKS: markings woven at exact intervals into the back of a patterned carpet which facilitate pattern matching and seaming.

MILLED DRUGGET: type of woven floor covering "painted in rich colours" introduced in America in the mid-19th century as an excellent carpet substitute for small rooms.

MOQUETTE: French term for velvet carpet applied to American-made Axminsters in the 1870s.

MOSAIC RUG: small fragile mid-19th century pictorial rug made by gluing backing on ends of specially arranged lengths of yarn and slicing off a cross section to produce a finished rug.

NAVAJO RUG: an extension of traditional Navajo Indian blanket weaving developed for trade purposes in the late 19th century.

OILCLOTH and **FLOOR OILCLOTH**: originally: cloth treated with oil and/or paint to make it durable and waterproof. Later: a floor covering of heavy canvas, jute or burlap, sized with glue, coated with several layers of thick oil paint, rubbed down with pumice, block-printed, varnished and rolled.

ORIENTAL REPRODUCTIONS: American machine-made Wilton or Axminster imitations of hand-made Persian and Turkish rugs; first made about 1900.

PAPER CARPET: carpet made of paper specially processed to produce a tough leather-like surface which was finished with wood grain or plain colors; used in hallways, hotel dining rooms and hospitals.

PARQUET/PARQUETRY: floors patterned with inlaid wood.

PILE: raised loops or tufts either cut or uncut which form the surface of various types of carpet: Axminster, chenille, Wilton, Brussels, shag, and hooked, among others.

PILE WEAVING: durable woven fabric having three sets of yarns, a warp and weft forming the foundation and the pile yarns which project at right angles from the foundation.

PITCH also GAUGE: a standard measure for woven carpets based on the number of ends of warp yarns contained in a 27 inch width.

PLANTING: method of increasing the number of colors in a Brussels/Wilton carpet by substituting bobbins of different colors in the frames rather than increasing the number of frames.

PLY: the number of single strand yarns twisted together to form a heavier, multi-strand yarn; also the descriptive term for the two and three layers of fabric interwoven to form ingrain carpeting.

POLYPROPYLENE: a synthetic material, woven and non-woven, impervious to moisture, shrinkage and mildew; used as primary and secondary backing for tufted, needle-punch and flocked carpets.

PRIMARY BACKING: woven or non-woven fabric into which pile yarns are tufted, sewn, or hooked. *See also* SECONDARY BACKING.

PROFILE WIRE: carpet wire with a contoured upper edge used to form a multi-level pile in velvet and Wilton carpets.

QUARTER: unit equalling 9 inches ($\frac{1}{4}$ yard) used to designate woven carpet widths in America. The standard 27 inch carpeting was known as $\frac{3}{4}$; others were referred to as $\frac{2}{4}$, $\frac{4}{4}$ and $\frac{12}{4}$.

RAVEL RUGS/RAVEL KNIT RUGS: 19th-century rugs with a shaggy pile formed by the raveled edges of scraps of knitted goods, stitched to a woven backing.

RAYON: a man-made cellulose fiber originally known as artificial silk; used in carpet manufacture especially as a durable carpet backing.

REED: the device on a loom containing numerous thin strips of reed or metal which separate and space the warp threads.

ROVING: a loose, slightly twisted rope of partially spun cotton or woolen fibers used as the filling in some rag carpets.

RESILIENT FLOORING: term for vinyl floorings which have replaced linoleum.

RUG: a floor covering of any size or material finished on all four sides that does not cover an entire floor and can be laid without being fastened down.

RUNNER: a long narrow floor covering used especially in halls, narrow passages and on stairs (stair runner).

RUSH: a swamp plant used for making matting.

SAXONY: luxurious high-pile Wilton first marketed in 1893.

SCATTER RUGS also THROW RUGS: 1930s term for small rugs that could be used at random on bare floors or with larger rugs.

SCRIM: loose woven core fabric in needlepunched carpet used to provide dimensional stability, and sometimes a second backing.

SCOTCH also KILMARNOCK: general name for flatwoven reversible carpets made in Scotland; also known as Kilmarnock after a specific weaving center where they were made. Equivalent of Kidderminster in England and ingrain in America.

SCULPTURED SURFACE: carpet surface carved with scissors or electric clippers to produce pattern and color variations through multiple levels.

SECONDARY BACKING: woven or non-woven material applied to the back of a tufted carpet to provide additional tuft bind, weight and dimensional stability.

SERGE: a durable twill fabric usually of worsted or worsted and wool used during the 19th century as a covering to protect good carpets from wear and soil.

SHADING: shifts in surface color characteristic of monochrome velvet carpets caused by footprints and cleaning.

SHAG CARPET: tufted carpet with relatively few tufts per inch of exceptionally long pile which falls at random in all directions to form the surface.

SHEARING: carpet finishing process in which spiral rotating blades trim the pile to a uniform height.

SHEDDING: a temporary condition in which short ends of fibers remaining in newly finished carpet work loose with wear and form lint balls on the surface.

SHEET VINYLS: vinyls manufactured in broadloom widths of 6, 9, 12 and 15 feet.

SHOTS: weft yarns which hold the pile of a woven carpet in place.

SHUTTLE: boat-shaped wooden bobbin holder which carries the weft across the warp from one side of the loom to the other.

SMYRNA RUGS: reversible chenille Axminster rugs in which the warp is cotton, the pattern weft chenille, and the filler is jute. A distinctively American form originated in Philadelphia in the 1870s, popular until the 1920s. Originally a Turkish rug shipped from Smyrna.

SPATTER LINOLEUM: inlaid linoleum pattern with multi-colored speckled effect resembling "spatter-dash" painted floors (about 1949).

SPOOL: bobbin the width of the loom containing all the colors for one crosswise row of Axminster carpet pattern.

SPROUTING: term for a hidden end of pile yarn working itself loose and appearing on the surface after a carpet has been installed.

STAIR: a term for a carpet width suitable for stairs used until the mid-20th century.

STAIR ROD/CARPET ROD: rod of brass, iron or wood which holds a stair carpet in place at the back of the tread. Lightweight 18th-century variety known as stair wire.

STITCHES/ROWS: measure of quality of tufted carpets based on the number of tufts in lengthwise inch.

STRAIGHT LINE INLAID: early continuously popular inlaid linoleum with simple, sharply delineated geometric patterns.

STRIP CARPET: narrow widths of carpet suitable for stairs or halls, or to be seamed together to make room-sized rugs.

STUFFERS: extra warp yarns, usually jute, which add weight, thickness and bulk to a pile-woven carpet.

TAPESTRY CARPETS: a pile carpet imitating Brussels and Wiltons invented in 1832 in which all the worsted yarns, preprinted with the pattern colors, are visible on the surface. Also Taps, Tapestry Brussels, Tapestry Velvets, and Velvets.

TILES: flat squares, usually 9 to 18 inches, installed individually to cover floors. Can be of stone, fire clay, matting, carpet, or resilient material such as asphalt composition, linoleum, cork, or rubber.

TUFT: a cut or uncut loop of surface yarn in woven or tufted carpet.

TUFTED CARPET: needle-stitched carpet in which the pile is produced by an adaptation of the multi-needle sewing machine.

VELVET: originally known as tapestry velvet. A cut-pile imitation of a Wilton weave made with a single set of pile yarns.

VENETIAN: inexpensive strip carpeting with a worsted warp concealing the weft; usually striped.

VINYL: durable transparent plastic often combined with pigments and fillers; developed in the 1940s and used as a basic material in the manufacture of resilient flooring.

WALL-TO-WALL: contemporary term for broadloom carpeting that is fitted and fastened down to cover the entire floor surface.

WARP: lengthwise yarns in a woven carpet that form the pattern and structure.

WEARLAYER: the color and pattern layer of linoleum or resilient flooring.

WEFT or FILLING or SHOTS: crosswise structural yarns which run from selvage to selvage to form the pattern or hold the pile in place.

WIRE: strip of metal over which the pattern warp is woven to form a pile. Also a term of quality indicating the number of rows of pile per lengthwise inch of carpet.

WILTON: cut-pile carpet woven on a Jacquard loom; colors in the pattern not appearing on the surface are carried in the structure of the carpet back until they are needed. Presently the term Wilton is used to define all carpets woven on a Jacquard loom including the looped pile formerly known as Brussels.

WOOLENS: short staple, soft wool with better felting quality than worsted; used for manufacture of less expensive carpets.

WORSTEDS: high quality long staple wools used to make the finest most expensive carpet yarns.

YARN-SEWN RUGS: late-18th- and early-19th-century geometric and pictorial rugs, embroidered in two-ply worsted wool in crewel stitches.

Bibliography

The American Domestic Cyclopaedia: A Volume of Universal Ready Reference for American Women in American Homes. New York: F. M. Lupton, 1890.

Amsden, Charles Avery. *Navajo Weaving.* Santa Ana, Calif.: The Fine Arts Press, 1934.

Andrews, Edward D. *The Community Industries of the Shakers.* Albany, N.Y.: The University of the State of New York, 1932.

Andrews, Edward D. and Faith. *Shaker Furniture: The Craftsmanship of an American Communal Sect.* New Haven: Yale University Press, and London: Dover Publications, 1937.

Bacon, Richard M. "The Painted Floor Pattern—A Colonial Original." *Yankee,* October 1975, pp. 82–9.

Baltimore Bargain House. *Price List of the Carpets.* Baltimore, Md.: 1908.

Beecher, Catherine E. and Harriet Beecher Stowe. *American Woman's Home.* 1869; Reprint ed., Hartford, Conn.: Stowe-Day Foundation, 1975.

Beecher, Mrs. W. H. *All Around the House,* New York: D. Appleton and Company, 1879.

Beitter, Ethyl Jane. *Hooked and Knotted Rugs.* Little Craft Book Series. New York: Sterling Publishing Co., Inc., 1973.

Bennet, Noel. *The Weaver's Pathway.* Flagstaff, Ariz.: Northland Press, 1974.

Bigelow Hartford Carpet Company. *A Century of Carpet and Rug Making in America, 1825-1925.* New York: 1925.

Black, A. and C. *Oriental Carpets, Runners and Rugs: and Some Jacquard Reproductions.* London: Adam and Charles Black, MCMX.

Bogdonoff, Nancy Dick. *Handwoven Textiles of Early New England.* Harrisburg, Pa.: Stackpole Books, 1975.

Bowles, Ella Shannon. *Handmade Rugs.* Boston: Little Brown & Co., 1927.

Burnham, Harold B. and Dorothy K. Burnham. *Keep Me Warm One Night: Early Handweaving in Eastern Canada.* Toronto: University of Toronto Press in co-operation with The Royal Ontario Museum, 1972.

Burt, S. H., ed. *What Every One Should Know: A Cyclopedia of Practical Information.* New York: A. L. Burt, 1888.

By One Who Knows. *How to Do Things Well and Cheap for Domestic Use.* Boston: Charles Tappan, 1845.

Carmichael, W. L.; Linton, George E. and Price, Isaac.

Calloway Textile Dictionary. LaGrange, Ga.: Callaway Mills, 1947.

The Carpet and Rug Institute. *Product Training School Manual.* Dalton, Ga.: The Carpet and Rug Institute, 1977.

The Carpet Trade. Published monthly by Berri & Brother. New York: 1875–1877.

Carson, Marian Sadtler. "Washington's American Carpet at Mount Vernon." *Antiques,* February 1947, pp. 118–119.

Chamberlain, Samuel and Flynt, Henry N. *Historic Deerfield: Houses and Interiors.* Revised edition. New York: Hastings House, 1972.

Chapman, Pat. "American Inventive Genius: Hooked Rugs to Broadloom." *Modern Floor Coverings,* July 1976, pp. 19–39.

Chapman, Pat. "10 Contemporary Carpet Giants Selected in MFC Poll." *Modern Floor Coverings,* August 1976, pp. 10–34.

Christensen, Erwin O. *The Index of American Design.* New York: Macmillan Co. for the National Gallery of Art, Smithsonian Institution, Washington, D.C., 1950.

Cole, Arthur and Williamson, Harold. *The American Carpet Manufacture: A History and an Analysis.* Cambridge: Harvard University Press, 1941.

Cole, Geo. S. *Cole's Encyclopedia of Dry Goods.* New edition revised and enlarged. New York: Root Newspaper Association, 1900.

Comstock, Helen. "Eighteenth Century Floor Cloths." *Antiques,* January 1955, p. 48.

"Contract Carpet: Selection and Specifications Guide." Dow/Badioche. Revision 4, September 1976.

Cook, Clarence. *House Beautiful.*

Cook, Clarence. *What Shall We Do with Our Walls?* New York: Warren, Fuller & Co., 1880.

Cooper, Grace Rogers. *The Copp Family Textiles.* Washington, D.C.: Smithsonian Institution Press, 1971.

Cox, Michael, "Through the Governor's Window." *El Palacio,* February 1974.

Cranbrook Academy of Art Exhibition Catalogue. "The Creative Spirit of Cranbrook: The Early Years." Bloomfield Hills, Mich: Cranbrook Academy of Art/ Museum, 1972.

Cutbush, James. *The American Artists Manual or Dictionary of Practical Knowledge.* Philadelphia: Johnson & Warner, and R. Fisher, 1814.

Cuyler, Susanne. *The High Pile Rug Book.* New York: Harper & Row, Publishers, Inc., 1974.

Dedera, Don. *Navajo Rugs; How to Find, Evaluate, Buy and Care for Them.* Flagstaff, Ariz.: Northland Press, 1975.

de Wolfe, Elsie. *The House in Good Taste*. New York: The Century Co., 1920.

Dilliard, Maud Esther. *An Album of New Netherland*. New York: Twayne Publishers, Inc., 1963.

Dockstadter, Frederick J. *Indian Art of the Americas*. New York Museum of the American Indian. Heye Foundation, 1973.

Dow, George Francis. *The Arts and Crafts in New England, 1704-1775*. Topsfield, Mass.: The Wayside Press, 1927.

Dow, George Francis. *Everyday Life in the Massachusetts Bay Colony*. Boston: The Society for the Preservation of New England Antiquities, 1935.

Drepperd, Carl W. *American Pioneer Arts and Artists*. Springfield, Mass.: The Pond-Ekberg Company, 1942.

Dry Goods Economist. "Exposition of American Retailing." New York: The Textile Publishing Co. Saturday 4 November 1899.

Dry Goods Economist. "World Wide Number." New York: The Textile Publishing Co. Saturday 4 April 1914.

Eastlake, Charles Licke. *Hints on Household Taste in Furniture, Upholstery and Other Details*. 1878; reprint ed., London and New York: Dover Publications, Inc., 1969.

Elliott, Charles Wyllys. *The Book of American Interiors*. Boston: James R. Osgood and Company, 1876.

Emery, Irene. *Roundtable on Museum Textiles, 1975 Proceedings*, ed. Patricia L. Fiske, Washington, D.C.: The Textile Museum, 1976.

Erdmann, Kurt. *Oriental Carpets*. New York: Universe Books, 1962.

Ewing, John S. and Norton, Nancy P. *Broadlooms and Businessmen: A History of the Bigelow-Sanford Carpet Company*. Cambridge: Harvard University Press, 1955.

N.A. "Family History Recorded in Rug." *Hobbies*, January 1950, p. 16.

Faraday, Cornelia B. *European and American Carpets and Rugs*. Grand Rapids, Mich: The Dean-Hicks Co., 1929.

Faude, W. "Associated Artists and the American Renaissance in the Decorative Arts." *Winterthur Portfolio 10*, 1975.

Faulkner, Ray and Sarah. *Inside Today's Home*. 3rd ed., New York: Holt, Rinehart and Winston, Inc. 1968.

Feeley, Helen Howard. *The Complete Book of Rug Braiding*. New York: Coward McCann, Inc., 1957.

Flint Institute of Art Exhibition Catalogue. *Art of the Great Lakes Indians*. Flint, Mich: Flint Institute of Arts, 1973.

Fraser, Esther Stevens. "Some Colonial and Early American Decorative Floors." *Antiques*, April 1931, pp. 296–301.

Frost, E. S. & Co. *Descriptive Circular: E. S. Frost & Co.'s Turkish Rug Patterns. Colored Rug or Mat Patterns*. 1884.

Gilroy, Clinton C. *The Art of Weaving by Hand and Power*. New York: George D. Baldwin, 1844.

Good Furniture Magazine: The Magazine of Decoration. Grand Rapids, Mich.: The Dean Hicks Company, Vol. XI, No. 3, September 1918.

Graybill & Co., *Catalogue of Graybill & Co.; Carpets and Oil Cloths, Wood and Willow Ware, Stationery, Grocers' Outfit, Varrets, Ec.*, n.d.

Greer, Michael. *Inside Design*. New York: Doubleday & Company, Inc., 1962.

Guild, Vera P. *Good Housekeeping, New Complete Book of Needlecraft*. New York: Book Club Edition. Good Housekeeping Books, 1971.

Hall, Philip A. *The Rug and Carpet Industry of Philadelphia*. Philadelphia: The Philadelphia Chamber of Commerce, 1917.

Hakanson, Joy. "Cranbrook." *Craft-Horizons*, Vol. XIX, No. 3 (May, June 1959), 18–20.

Hartley, Miss Florence. *The Ladies' Hand Book of Fancy and Ornamental Work*. Philadelphia: J. W. Bradley, Publisher, 1859.

Hartshorne, Henry. *The Household Cyclopedia of General Information Containing Over Ten Thousand Recipes in All the Useful and Domestic Arts*. Philadelphia: Baker, Davis & Co., 1876.

Henderson, Philip. *William Morris: His Life, Work and Friends*. New York: McGraw-Hill Book Co., 1967.

Hicks, Amy Mali. *The Craft of Hand-made Rugs*. New York: Empire State Book Company, 1936.

Higley, Mary Gerrish. "The Caswell Carpet." *Antiques*, June 1926, pp. 396–8.

N.A. *Household Conveniences*. New York: Orange Judd Co., 751 Broadway, 1884.

How to Lay and Care for Linoleum. Lancaster, Pa.: Armstrong Cork Co. Linoleum Dept., 1918.

Hubel, Reinhard G. *The Book of Carpets*. New York, Washington: Praeger Publishers, London: Barrie & Jenkins, 1970.

Hughes, G. Bernard. "The Englishness of Turkey-Work," *Country Life*, 11 February 1965, pp. 309–10.

Jacobs, Bertram. *Axminster Carpets (hand made) 1755-1957*. Leigh-on-Sea, England: F. Lewis, Publishers, Ltd., 1970.

Jaray, Madeleine. *The Carpets of the Manufacture de la Savonnerie*. Leigh-on-Sea, England: F. Lewis, Publishers, Ltd., 1966.

Johnson, Theodore E. *Hands to Work and Hearts to God: The Shaker Tradition in Maine*. Bath, Maine: Bowdoin College Museum of Art, 1969.

Kent, William Winthrop. *Rare Hooked Rugs*. Springfield, Mass.: The Pond-Ekberg Co., 1941.

Kent, William Winthrop. *The Hooked Rug*. New York: Mead & Co., 1930.

Kent, William Winthrop. *Hooked Rug Design*. Springfield, Mass.: The Pond Ekberg Co., 1941.

Kenyon, Otis Allen. *Carpets and Rugs*. North Canton, Ohio: The Hoover Rug Company, 1923.

Keyes, Homer Eaton. "A Note on Embroidered Carpets." *Antiques*, June 1926, pp. 398–402.

Kimball, Marie G. "The Furnishing of Governor Penn's House." *Antiques*, May 1931, pp. 375–8.

Kirk, Robert W. *Carpet Industry: Present Status and Future Prospects*. Philadelphia: Wharton Miscellaneous Series No. 17, 1970.

Klamkin, Marian. *Hands to Work: Shaker Folk Art and Industries*. New York: Dodd, Mead & Company, 1972.

Kocher, A. Lawrence. *Floor . . . Floor Cloth . . . Carpets: In 17th-18th Century Architectural Meaning and Usage*. Unpublished research report from the Research Archives of the Colonial Williamsburg Foundation, Williamsburg, Va.: 1945.

Kopp, Joel and Kate. *American Hooked and Sewn Rugs*. New York: E. P. Dutton & Co., Inc., 1975.

Kron, Joan. "Splendor of the Grass: Straw Rugs." *New York Magazine*, 3 June 1974, pp. 78–80.

Lambert, Miss. *The Hand-Book of Needlework*. New York: Wiley & Putnam, 161 Broadway, 1842.

Landreau, Anthony N. *America Underfoot: A History of Floor Coverings from Colonial Times to the Present*. Washington, D.C.: published for the Smithsonian Institution Traveling Exhibition Service by the Smithsonian Institution Press, 1976.

Lanier, Mildred B. *English and Oriental Carpets at Williamsburg*. Williamsburg, Va.: The Colonial Williamsburg Foundation, 1975.

Leslie, Frank. *Frank Leslie's Illustrated Historical Register of the Centennial Exposition 1876*. Reprint ed., New York: Paddington Press Ltd., 1974.

Lichten, Frances. *Folk Art of Rural Pennsylvania*. New York: Charles Scribner's Sons, 1946.

Lipman, Jean and Winchester, Alice. *The Flowering of American Folk Art, 1776-1876*. New York: Viking Press, 1974.

Little, Nina Fletcher. *American Decorative Wall Painting, 1700-1850*. London and New York.

Little, Nina Fletcher. "Floor Coverings." *The American Art Journal*, Vol. VII, No. 1 (May 1975), 107–18.

Little, Nina Fletcher. *Floor Coverings in New England before 1850*. Second printing, Sturbridge, Mass.: Old Sturbridge Village, 1972.

Little, Nina Fletcher. *Paintings by New England Provincial Artists 1775-1800*. Boston; Museum of Fine Arts, 1976.

Lyford, Carrie A. *Ojibwa Crafts*. Phoenix, Ariz.; Department of the Interior, Bureau of Indian Affairs, 1953.

Lynes, Russell. *The Tastemakers*. New York: Grosset & Dunlap, The Universal Library, 1954.

Lyman, Joseph B. and Laura E. *The Philosophy of Housekeeping: A Scientific and Practical Manual*. Hartford, Conn.: Goodwin and Betts, 1867.

Maass, John. *The Victorian Home in America*. New York: Hawthorn Books, Inc., 1972.

"The Manufacture of Floorcloth." *The Carpet Trade*, Vol. 17, No. 1 (October 1875), pp. 13–14.

McMullan, Joseph V. "The Turkey Carpet in Early America." *Antiques*, March 1954, pp. 220–1.

Meader, Robert F. W. *Illustrated Guide to Shaker Furniture*, London and New York: Dover Publications, Inc., 1972.

Melcher, Marguerite Fellows. *The Shaker Adventure*. Princeton, New Jersey; Princeton University Press, 1941.

Mellon, Gertrude A. and Wilder, Elizabeth F., eds. *Maine and Its Role in American Art 1740-1963*. A Studio Book, New York: The Viking Press, 1963.

Mera, H. P. *Southwestern Textiles: The Alfred I. Barton Collection*. Santa Fe, N.M.: San Vincente Foundation, Inc., 1949.

Miles, Charles. "Mat Making: North American Indian Mats." *Hobbies*, September 1973, pp. 142–7.

Montgomery Ward & Co. Catalogue No. 57. *Catalogue and Buyer's Guide, Spring and Summer 1895* (unabridged facsimile). London and New York: Dover Publications, 1969.

Museum of American Folk Art Exhibition Catalogue. *Hooked Rugs in the Folk Art Tradition*, New York: Museum of American Folk Art, 1974.

"The New Carpet Fabrics of the 19th Century." *The Carpet Trade*, Vol. 7, No. 4, (January 1876), p. 12.

New York Interiors at the Turn of the Century. Photographs by Joseph Byron from the Byron Collection of the Museum of the City of New York, New York: Dover Publications, Inc., 1976.

The New York Magazine or Literary Repository for June 1791. Vol. 11, No. 4, New York: Printed by Thomas and James Swords, No. 27 William Street, MDCCXCI, pp. 311–32.

O'Brien, Mildred Jackson. *The Rug and Carpet Book*.

New York: M. Barrows and Company, Inc., 1946.

Osborne, Harold. *The Oxford Companion to the Decorative Arts.* Oxford, England: The Clarendon Press, 1975.

Page, Ruth. "English Carpets and Their Use in America." *The Connecticut Antiquarian: The Bulletin of the Antiquarian and Landmarks Society Inc., of Connecticut.* Vol. XIX, No. 1 (June 1967), pp. 16–25.

Parsons, Frank Alvah. *The Art of Home Furnishing and Decoration.* Lancaster, Pa.: Armstrong Cork Company Linoleum Dept., 1918.

Patmore, Derek. *Color Schemes and Modern Furnishing.* New York and London: The Studio, 1945.

Pendleton, Mary. *Navajo and Hopi Weaving Techniques.* New York: Macmillan Publishing Co., Inc., 1974.

Peterson, Harold L. *Americans at Home: from the Colonists to the Late Victorians.* New York: Charles Scribner's Sons, 1971.

Pettes, H. & Co. *Elegant Brussels and Royal Wilton Carpetings.* Boston.

Philadelphia—A Story of Progress. New York: Lewis Historical Publishing Co., 1941.

Prime, Alfred Coxe. *The Arts and Crafts in Philadelphia, Maryland and South Carolina 1721-1785.* Topsfield, Mass.: The Walpole Society, 1929.

Prime, Alfred Coxe. *The Arts and Crafts in Philadelphia, Maryland and South Carolina 1786-1800.* Series 2, Topsfield, Mass.: The Walpole Society, 1932.

Quinn, Richard L. *Carpets and Rugs.* North Canton, Ohio: The Hoover Home Institute, 1976.

Robacker, Earl F. *Pennsylvania Dutch Stuff.* Philadelphia: University of Pennsylvania Press, 1961.

Ross, E. & Co. *Manufacturers of Rug Patterns and Machines Catalogue.* Toledo City, Ohio, 1889.

Roth, Rodris. *Floor Coverings in 18th Century America.* United States National Museum Bulletin 250, Paper 59. Washington, D.C.: Smithsonian Institution, 1967.

Scobey, Joan. *Rugs and Wall Hangings.* Marjorie Sablow, illus., New York: The Dial Press, 1974.

Sears, Roebuck and Company Catalogue No. 111, 1902, reprinted. New York: Crown Publishers, Inc., 1969.

Sears, Roebuck Catalogue, Spring and Summer, 1927.

Sears, Roebuck Catalogue, Fall and Winter, 1974.

"The Slim Look in Rugs." *Look,* 2 April 1957.

Stauffer, Elmer C. "In the Pennsylvania Dutch Country." *National Geographic Magazine,* Vol. 80 (July–December 1941), pp. 37–74.

N.A. *The Story of the Sloanes.* New York: W. & J. Sloane, 1950.

Spinden, Herbert J. "The Navajo and His Blanket." *Craft Horizons,* August 1945, pp. 10–35.

"The Story of American Needlework," reprint from *Woman's Day Magazine* (October 1961), New York: Fawcett Publications.

Swygert, Mrs. Arthur M., ed. *Heirlooms from Old Looms.* A catalogue of coverlets owned by the Colonial Coverlet Guild of America and its members, revised ed. Chicago: privately printed, 1955.

Tattersall, C. E. C. *A History of British Carpets,* revised by Stanley Reed. Leigh-on-Sea, England: F. Lewis Publishers, Ltd., 1966.

Taussig, F. W. *The Tariff History of the United States.* New York: G. P. Putnam's Sons, 1892.

Tomlinson, Charles. "The Manufacture of Carpets." *The Useful Art and Manufactures of Great Britain,* first series. London: n.d., pp. 8–9.

Van der Donk, Adriaen. *A Description of the New Netherlands.* Syracuse, N.Y.: Syracuse University Press, 1968.

Vantine, A. A. & Co. *Oriental Carpets, Rugs and Embroideries.* New York.

Wadsworth Atheneum Catalogue. *Bed Rugs 1722-1833.* Hartford, Conn.: Wadsworth Atheneum, 1975.

Wagner, Dorothy and Houseman, Robert W. *What You Should Know About Carpet.* New York: Popular Library, 1967.

Wainwright, Nicholas B. *Colonial Grandeur in Philadelphia: The House and Furniture of General John Cadwalader.* Philadelphia: The Historical Society of Pennsylvania, 1964.

Webster, T. and Mrs. Parkes. *The American Family Encyclopedia of Useful Knowledge.* New York: Derby & Jackson, 119 Nassau Street, 1858.

Weeks, Jeanne G. and Treganowan, Donald. *Rugs and Carpets of the Western World.* London and Philadelphia: Chilton Book Co., 1969.

Whaley, Peggy. "Bicentennial Tribute: Reviewing the History of the Tufting Industry." *Carpet and Rug Industry.* July 1976, pp. 12–13.

Wheat, Joseph Ben. *Navajo Blankets,* from the collection of Anthony Berlant. University of Arizona Museum of Art, 1974.

"What is an 'Ingrain'?" *The Carpet Trade,* Vol. 7, No. 3 (December 1875), p. 17.

Wheeler, Candace. *How to Make Rugs.* New York: Doubleday, Page & Company, 1900.

Whiteford, Andrew Hunter. *North American Indian Arts.* New York: Golden Press, 1970.

Znamierowski, Nell. *Step by Step Rugmaking.* New York: Golden Press, London: Pan Books, 1972.

List of Color Illustrations and Picture Acknowledgements

Permission to reproduce black-and-white photographs has kindly been given by the following. Photographs on pages 174–7 are numbered in alphabetical order from left to right across each page.

Abby Aldrich Rockefeller Folk Art Center, Williamsburg, Virginia: 105 (bottom). Courtesy of The American Museum of Natural History, New York: 15, 16 (both). Courtesy of Armstrong Cork Company, Lancaster, Pennsylvania: 61, 63, 64 (bottom), 69, 70 (bottom). Reproduced from *The Art of Weaving by Hand and Power* by Clinton C. Gilroy: 73, 92. Courtesy of Bigelow-Sanford Inc., Greenville, South Carolina: 79, 80, 135, 146, 161 (bottom left), 176g, 176o, 177j, 177k, 177m, 177n, 177q. The Brooklyn Museum, Brooklyn, New York: 91 (top), gift of Mrs Caroline Weldy Marsteller; 121 (both), 174g (Scalamandré reproduction), 176b. The Byron Collection, Museum of the City of New York: 131 (top), 141. Reproduced from *Cole's Encyclopedia of Dry Goods*: 96. Congoleum Corporation, Kearney, New Jersey: 70 (top), 71 (both). Colonial Williamsburg Foundation, Williamsburg, Virginia: 133 (top), 148, 174c. Courtesy of Cobble Tufting Equipment, Chattanooga, Tennessee: 145 (bottom). Cranbrook Academy of Art, Bloomfield Hills, Michigan: 162, 163. Courtesy of Crossley Carpets, Halifax, England: 177i. Courtesy of the DAR Museum, Washington, D.C., gift of Mrs Tscharner D. Watkins: 142. Dartmouth College Museum and Galleries, Hanover, New Hampshire: 91 (bottom). Detroit Historical Museum, Detroit, Michigan: 33. Detroit Historical Society, Detroit, Michigan: 175g. Reproduced from the

Dry Goods Economist, 1918: 131 (bottom). Marguerite T. Frederick: 143. Reproduced from *Good Furniture Magazine*: 22, 111. Collections of Greenfield Village and the Henry Ford Museum, Dearborn, Michigan: 40, 151 (bottom). Courtesy of Hancock Village Shaker Museum, Hancock, Massachusetts: 47. Heritage Rugs, Lahaska, Pennsylvania: 31 (top). The Hermitage, Ho-Ho-Kus, New Jersey: 26. Historic Cherry Hill, Albany, New York: 58, 59 (both). Historical Society of Pennsylvania, Philadelphia, Pennsylvania: 52, 113. Independence National Historic Park Collection, Philadelphia, Pennsylvania: 134. Indianapolis Museum of Art, Indiana: 176e. Urban Jupena: 166. Reproduced from the *Ladies' Hand Book of Fancy and Ornamental Work*: 154, 155. Nicholas Langhart: 34 (left above). Jack Lenor Larsen Inc., New York: 123 (all). Courtesy of Bernard and S. Dean Levy Inc., New York: 29 (bottom). Courtesy The Magee Carpet Company, Bloomsburg, Pennsylvania: 77, 78, 136, 147 (right). Collection of Marilyn and Jim Marinacio, New York: 44 (bottom), photo courtesy of America Hurrah, New York. Courtesy of The Mariners Museum of Newport News, Virginia: 156. Merrimac Valley Textile Museum, North Andover, Massachusetts: 81, 174p, 175e, 175f, 175p, 176c, 176h, 176n, 176p. Metropolitan Museum of Art, New York: 152 (top), gift of Miss Isabelle Mygatt, 1923; 152 (bottom), gift of Katherine Keyes, 1938, in memory of her father Homer Eaton Keyes; 174d, 174h, 175b, 175d, 175o. Miami Purchase Association for Historic Preservation, John Hauck House, Cincinnati, Ohio: 14 (bottom); Sharon Woods Village, Cincinnati, Ohio: 174j, 174k. Courtesy of Mohawk Carpet, New York: 145 (top). Morris County Historical Society, Morristown, New Jersey: 117 (bottom), 177r. Museum of Fine Arts, Boston, gift of Mrs Horatio A. Lamb in memory of Mr and Mrs Winthrop Sargent: 53. Museum of Modern Art, New York, Edgar Kaufmann, Jr. Fund: 165. Collections of the Museum of New Mexico, Santa Fe, gift of Mrs Truman J. Mathews: 107. The Museums at Stony Brook, Stony Brook, New York: 101, 114, 176i. National Gallery of Art, Washington, gift of Edgar William and Bernice Chrysler Garbisch: 11 (top). National

Gallery of Ireland, Dublin: 133 (bottom). National Park Service, Appomattox, Virginia: 100 (bottom). Courtesy of the New York Historical Society, New York City: 11 (bottom). Courtesy of the New York State Historical Association, Cooperstown: 11 (center), 174e, 174i, 174l, 175m, 175n, 176d, 176k, 176m. *Color Schemes and Modern Furnishing* by Derek Patmore: 122. William Penn Memorial Museum, Pennsylvania Historical and Museum Commission, Harrisburg, Pennsylvania: 31 (bottom). Pennsylvania Farm Museum of Landis Valley, Lancaster, Philadelphia: 21 (both). Philadelphia Carpet Company, Cartersville, Georgia: 177s. Philadelphia Museum of Art, given by Mrs Edward M. Davis: 28, 74; purchased with funds donated by the Barra Foundation: 174o; purchased by the American Art Committee: 175a; given by Robert L. McNeil Junior Fund: 175j; purchased with funds donated by the Barra Foundation: 176a. Private Collection: 20; 29 (top), photo courtesy of America Hurrah, New York; 32, 39 (above right); 48 (top), photo courtesy of America Hurrah, New York; 60, 75, 100 (top), 102 (bottom), 161 (top left and right), 175c. Royal Ontario Museum, Toronto, Canada, gift of Mrs H. B. Burnham: 93, 95, 105 (top). Courtesy of Scalamandré Silks, New York: 174m. Courtesy of George E. Schoellkopf Gallery, New York: 42 (top). Courtesy Sears, Roebuck and Co., Chicago, Illinois: 23. Shaker Museum, Old Chatham, New York: 49. Shakertown at Pleasant Hill Inc., Harrisburg, Kentucky: 50. Shelburne Museum Inc., Shelburne, Vermont: 12 (top), 39 (above left), 82, 151 (top), 153. Courtesy of Sleepy Hollow Restorations, Tarrytown, New York: 13 (bottom), 175k, 177f, 177g, 177h. W & J Sloane Inc., New York: 25, 147 (left). Smithsonian Institution, Washington, D.C.: 102 (top), 104, 118, 132, 174a, 174b, 175h, 175i, 176f, 176j, 176l. Courtesy of The Speedwell Village, Morristown, New Jersey: 14 (top), 174n. The Taft Museum, Cincinnati, Ohio: 177o, 177p. Toledo Museum of Art, Toledo, Ohio: 117 (top). Victoria and Albert Museum, London, Crown copyright: 54 (both), 177a, 177b, 177c, 177d, 177e. Courtesy of V'Soske Inc., New York: 164 (bottom). Yale University Art Gallery, New Haven, Connecticut: 175l, 177l. Wadsworth Atheneum, Hartford,

Connecticut: 149. The Walters Art Gallery, Baltimore, Maryland: 129. George Wells, the Ruggery, Glen Head, New York: 164 (top left and right). Collection of Joseph and Ellen Wetherell, New York: 34 (left below and right); 41, photo courtesy of America Hurrah, New York; 48 (bottom). Courtesy The Henry Francis du Pont Winterthur Museum Libraries, Winterthur, Delaware: 42 (bottom), 43, 44 (top), 45 (both), 174f.

Photographs listed below were specially taken for the book by the following (color illustrations are indicated by italic type).

Author: 14 (both), 15, 16 (both), 22, 23, 31 (top), 34 (all), 39 (above right), 40, 47, 48 (bottom), *66, 73, 80, 86*, 92, 100 (top), 101, 102, 111, 114, 122, 131 (bottom), 143, 151 (bottom), 154, 155, *159*, 166, 174b, 174j, 174k, 174l, 174n, 175c, 175h, 175i, 175m, 176f, 176g, 176i, 176l, 176m, 176o, 177m, 177q, 177r. Mel Wathen, New York: 20, 31 (bottom), 32, *38, 56*, 60, *88, 97*, 102 (bottom), 117 (bottom), 161 (top left and right). James A. Viola, Detroit, Michigan: 26, 33, 162, 163, 175g.

The drawings are by Ann George. Those listed below were adapted from the sources mentioned. Details of publications are given in the bibliography.

Courtesy of *The Magazine Antiques*, New York: 12, 13 (top). Courtesy of Armstrong Cork Company, Lancaster, Pennsylvania: 64 (top). Kopp, Joel and Kate, *American Hooked and Sewn Rugs*: 40a, b, c, 46 (center), 150 (both). Courtesy of *The Craft Horizons Magazine*, August 1944, New York: 109. Courtesy of the Hoover Company, North Canton, Ohio (*Carpet & Rugs*): 83 (bottom), 124. C. E. C. Tattersall, *The History of British Carpets*: 75, 76, 77, 82 (both), 83 (top), 89 (both). The Torrington Company, Torrington, Connecticut: 83 (margin), 84 (margin).

The drawing on page 81 is by Werner H. Von Rosenstiel.

Endpapers: detail from the Pliney Moore carpet as shown on page 152. Metropolitan Museum of Art, New York, gift of Miss Isabelle Mygatt, 1923.

Index